BRIGHT NOTES

CATCH-22 BY JOSEPH HELLER

Intelligent Education

Nashville, Tennessee

BRIGHT NOTES: Catch-22
www.BrightNotes.com

No part of this publication may be used or reproduced in any manner whatsoever without written permission, except in the case of brief quotations in critical articles and reviews. For permissions, contact Influence Publishers http://www.influencepublishers.com.

ISBN: 978-1-645422-94-5 (Paperback)
ISBN: 978-1-645422-95-2 (eBook)

Published in accordance with the U.S. Copyright Office Orphan Works and Mass Digitization report of the register of copyrights, June 2015.

Originally published by Monarch Press.
Walter James Miller; Bonnie E. Nelson, 1955
2019 Edition published by Influence Publishers.

Interior design by Lapiz Digital Services. Cover Design by Thinkpen Designs.

Printed in the United States of America.

Library of Congress Cataloging-in-Publication Data forthcoming.
Names: Intelligent Education
Title: BRIGHT NOTES: Catch-22
Subject: STU004000 STUDY AIDS / Book Notes

CONTENTS

1) Introduction to Joseph Heller — 1

2) Themes — 18

3) Textual Analysis —
   Chapters 1–5 — 25
   Chapters 6–14 — 41
   Chapters 15–24 — 58
   Chapters 25–39 — 74

4) Characterization — 96

5) Character Analysis — 102

6) Critics Catch on to Catch-22 — 130

7) Essay Questions and Model Answers — 147

8) Topics for Research and Criticism — 156

9) Bibliography — 163

INTRODUCTION TO JOSEPH HELLER

JOSEPH HELLER AND CATCH-22

On several counts, *Catch-22* must be viewed as an extraordinary phenomenon. Although it is profound in its conception, complex in its artistry, and radical in its message, it has nevertheless very quickly become a popular classic. It has helped prepare the American public for entirely new kinds of art. In a period notorious for its "generation gap," *Catch-22* has earned renown among both older and younger readers. And so it has become the first literary classic that can actually be assigned to students with their enthusiastic approval!

HELLER'S YOUTH AND COMBAT SERVICE

"Everything I know is in *Catch-22*," Heller told the authors of this Note. "Everything" seems to include not only his extensive reading, which supplied the novel's many literary allusions, but also the lessons of his combat experience, and even memories of pre-war situations which figure prominently in the story. For Heller, born in 1923, grew up in a bleak neighborhood in the Coney Island section of Brooklyn, not far from Manhattan where Colonel Cargill presumably was "working," or from Staten Island where "Doc" Daneeka was "practicing." After

Heller was graduated from high school, he earned fifteen or sixteen dollars a week as a file clerk. The "Great Depression" was at its greatest and young Heller saw no chance at all of getting to college. After Pearl Harbor, he enlisted at the age of 19 in the Army Air Corps and was later commissioned and sent overseas as a bombardier. His outfit was based on Corsica in the Mediterranean.

"I was gung-ho for combat," he recalls, and he saw his share of it. Then one day - over Avignon - a man in his plane was wounded in the leg.

"He didn't die in my arms, the way a certain national magazine misrepresented it," Heller told us. "But it was bad enough." It made Heller think seriously for the first time about the meaning and nature of war.

HELLER'S EDUCATION

"I am, though, one of those who benefited from war. If I had not gone to war, I would not have gone to college." World War II veterans were able to earn their degrees under the educational provisions of the "GI Bill." "If I had not gone to college, I would not have been a writer. I don't know what would have become of me."

He studied at New York University where he especially enjoyed literature. One course he recalls with great pleasure is Greek Drama. "Reading Euripides' Bacchae gave me the background for the 'guzzling saturnalia' in the Thanksgiving scene." After he took his degree, he went to Oxford for a year on a Fulbright Fellowship. "Reading Shakespeare's *Julius Caesar* and Plutarch's *Lives* gave me ideas for the scene in which Dobbs talks of assassinating Cathcart. You see, everything I know is in *Catch-22*!"

WORK BEGINS ON "CATCH-18"

Back home, he published some short stories in magazines, then taught composition and literature for two years (1950–1952) at Pennsylvania State University, and finally became a full-time advertising copy-writer in New York. He had read Norman Mailer's *The Naked and the Dead* and James Jones' *From Here to Eternity* and kept thinking about writing his own war novel. The real inspiration came one night as he was reading Louis-Ferdinand Celine's *Journey to the End of Night*. "What I got from Celine is the right way to use the vernacular - my own language - and a sense of relaxed continuity." Five weeks later he started "Catch-18," as he called it. He wrote the first draft of Chapter One in one night, then spent a week revising it. His agent placed it with New World Writing.

During the year that it took New World Writing to get Chapter One (then titled "Catch-18") into print, Heller filled loose-leaf book after loose-leaf book with notes and outlines. Then he began the actual writing and worked at it two hours a night, five nights a week, for six years. "I was much aware of T. S. Eliot's *The Waste Land* as I wrote. Notice that Yossarian fears death by water. I even had "Those are pearls that were his eyes' in the first draft." Heller used religious and cultural **allusions** and parallels with great deliberation throughout. "Notice the similarity between the setting in the Old Man's apartment and the Venusburg set in Wagner's *Tannhauser*," he remarked to us. But for all the deliberate cultural apparatus, for all the careful outlining of complex time arrangements, he wanted most of all, he says, "to write something entertaining."

PUBLISHING HISTORY

Heller's title, *Catch-18*, had to be changed. An established novelist, Leon Uris (*Exodus*), had announced a novel called *Mila 18*. To avoid confusion, Heller's editor at Simon and Schuster called his new novelist's first book *Catch-22*. In its hard-cover format, issued in October 1961, *Catch-22* actually sold 35,000 copies in one year, a good sale for any "first novel." But since these sales were concentrated in the metropolitan New York area, the book did not "make" the best-seller lists which are based on national distribution of sales.

In England, though, *Catch-22*, hit the Number One spot on the best seller list just one week after its publication by Jonathan Cape. In September, 1962, Dell published the American paperback edition, two million copies of which had been sold by 1968. Delta also published a high-priced paperback version, and then *Catch-22* was issued in the prestigious Modern Library format, to put the sales figures close to four million copies by 1971. By then many schools had made *Catch-22* part of their "World Literature" reading-lists: in some colleges it is studied as the modern counterweight to Homer's *Iliad*. And, as we shall see ("Critics Catch on to *Catch-22*"), by then many leading critics and scholars had published major studies of *Catch-22*.

HELLER AS PLAYWRIGHT

Meanwhile, Heller himself had turned to writing for the stage. His *We Bombed in New Haven* was tried out at the Yale Drama School in New Haven and opened on Broadway on October 16, 1968. An extension, in many ways, of *Catch-22*, the play made it quite clear that Heller is now opposed to all war. "Anybody who enjoys war deserves war. Anybody who likes peace deserves freedom," he was quoted as saying to the New York Times. "When you go into service you give away the freedom that the Constitution forbids the government to take away from you."

We Bombed in New Haven earned high praise from *Newsweek*, *Life*, and other periodicals, but most serious students of literature still felt that Heller's talents are better realized in fiction. Nevertheless, when we interviewed him in the "Italian Pavilion," a restaurant in New York City, on June 11, 1971, he talked fondly and at length about a new play he was then revising. He had thought of calling it *The Hunt for Washington Irving*. But a few weeks later it was produced simply as *Catch-22*. It was well received by several critics when it ran for a two-week tryout in East Hampton, Long Island, in July 1971.

CATCH-22 AS FILM

Mike Nichols had directed and released in mid-1970, a film version of *Catch-22* which drew mixed feelings from critics. Nichols tried to approximate the "spiral" structure of the novel, circling back three times to Snowden's death. The disadvantage of this format is that it gives the impression that the Snowden trauma is the main reason for Yossarian's desertion. "But," as Richard Schickel complained, "it was one of dozens of incidents, exchanges, imaginings that ... made him mad and then made him run for his sanity. To simplify him so radically is to betray him as a human being and to betray that complexity of version, that vigorous and skillful art, which gave *Catch-22* the powerful hold it has exercised on a generation."

SOMETHING HAPPENED

During the years when he appeared to be concerned mainly with play and film, Heller actually was working on his second novel, *Something Happened*, scheduled for publication in 1972. This is the story of a man employed by a large company who hopes to work himself up to the point where he is the one chosen to deliver the speech at the company's annual **convention** in Bermuda. "He knows all the time that this is a rather specious ambition," Heller tells us, "but still - that's his ambition." In the writing, Heller has been influenced, on the one hand, by Kafka, and on the other, by Bob Dylan. "I like Dylan's method - it's elliptical, it's connotative. And I'm thinking of using some of his lines - like 'Something's happening, and you don't know what it is, do you, Mr. Jones? - as my superscription."

Heller says that the main character of *Something Happened* is "the opposite of Yossarian, twenty years later."

"Do any recollections of the war figure in this novel?," we asked.

Heller thought a minute. "There's a nine-year old boy watching an old war movie on television." Then Joseph Heller left the "Italian Pavilion" to meet his wife and two children.

HELLER'S THEMES, INFLUENCES, AND TECHNIQUES

Catch-22 is one of the most intricately designed and ramified works in world literature. Its structure is complex; its cast of characters is legion. And as its story unfolds and its major characters develop, there emerges too a pattern of interrelated **themes** rendered in a great variety of literary techniques. Properly appreciated, *Catch-22* finally impresses the reader as being a great artistic statement of man's condition comparable to Homer's *Iliad*, Dante's *Inferno*, or Joyce's *Finnegans Wake*.

In the detailed textual analysis that follows this section, we shall see that Heller's story ultimately explores what we may, for convenience's sake, identify as:

TEN MAJOR THEMES

1. War is a corrosively immoral, absurd, and cynical activity whose ultimate effect is to create chaos favorable for powermad manipulators and exploiters.

2. Modern war hastens the mechanization and depersonalization already fostered by modern society.

3. Abstract goals and functions - rather than human aims and life-loving processes - characterize modern life. Good examples are bureaucratic record-keeping, adherence to unexamined beliefs, faith in sophistical rationality. That these abstractions are likely to be false and used for anti-human purposes is powerfully stated early in the novel (p. 16 in Dell paperback):

All over the world, boys ... were laying down their lives for what they had been told was their country.

4. Our institutions and professions are corrupt and our declared aims, in peace and war, are hypocritical.

5. Communications have broken down, between person and person, and between institution and individual.

6. Man is alienated from his own body, his own feelings, and his own nature.

7. As a consequence of 2. to 6., expressed in their worst form through 1., most people are in a state of confusion and anxiety.

8. God is dead.

9. Those few people who have been able to maintain any sensitivity and perspective have had to realize that there is a Higher Morality than the State. (This Higher Morality may resurrect even God!)

10. All of these conditions mean that there is a critical need for a New Hero.

In the detailed textual and character analyses that follow this section, we shall see that these **themes** are introduced, varied and studied from many angles through Heller's skillful use of both conventional and special literary techniques.

SATIRE

Heller uses a variety of literary modes: the satirical, the surrealistic, and the realistic. One of the main proofs of his literary genius is his blending and variation of these modes to achieve his unique effects. **Satire** is a literary manner that uses wit, **irony**, and sarcasm to expose and discredit human follies and vices. It is, of course, the humor that makes the bitter moral palatable. Heller's humor makes us drop our guard for the serious blow to follow. **Black Humor**, always a tactic with good writers, becomes a major technique with Heller. It may be defined as a bitter emphasis on the absurd that makes us laughs so that we will not cry. "I wanted," Heller once said in a Mademoiselle interview, "people to laugh and then look back with horror at what they were laughing at."

SURREALISM

From the satirical. Heller is likely to go to the surrealistic, which is to say, dreamlike experience treated as if it were "really" happening. In dreams, facts and feelings are distorted and exaggerated. A person who knows a soldier like Milo Minderbinder - i.e., a soldier willing to make a profit out of war - may feel that really Milo's activities are aiding the enemy. This person could symbolize this feeling by dreaming that Milo has bombed his own squadron. But in Heller's surrealistic treatment, the characters are living that experience. Of course, Heller's use of surrealism adds to his **satire**: real life is as nightmarish as any sick, delirious dream.

REALISM

Heller will abruptly go from satirical or surrealistic exaggeration to outright **realism**, which is to say, the kind of reporting of events that is basically an audio-visual recording of outer reality. Again, Heller's themes are reinforced by the fact that these utterly credible situations (Snowden's outpouring of intestines, the dark secrets of Rome at night) are just as horrendous as any nightmarish or satirical distortion.

STRUCTURE

Heller structures his material - that is, arranges his revelations - in a psychological fashion. The experience that he wishes to communicate to us is revealed largely by free association. Present action evokes recollections of past actions which are then experienced in artistic simultaneity. We are introduced to this technique immediately. On the first page, we hear about Yossarian and the Chaplain. Then the narrative spirals off on a rapid series of free associations, returning four pages later to Yossarian and the Chaplain. But other bits introduced into Chapter One may not materialize for 70 or 100 pages later. Some motifs - like the Snowden trauma - will spiral back into our awareness again and again, with something new each time. Thus a pattern of **foreshadowings** and echoes is set up, and it is reinforced by such symbolic situations as that of the Soldier who Saw Everything Twice and that of the Chaplain who ponders paramnesia (the illusory sensation that one has experienced present circumstances before). An important element in this pattern is contrast. Heller, as we shall see, uses contrasts of all kinds: in mood, characterization, setting, situation, language.

SETTING

The novel apparently takes place on the Island of Pianosa, eight miles south of Elba in the Mediterranean. The real Pianosa is too small to accommodate all the actions, places, and population of *Catch-22*. The fictitious Pianosa takes on a mythic quality. It is the psychological "home base" of men who experience orgies and nightmares on the "mainland" (Rome, for example) and incredible horrors in the air. Two settings on Pianosa take on, as we shall see, special symbolic significance: Yossarian's tent and the hospital to which he frequently escapes.

CHARACTERIZATION

Heller uses virtually all the known techniques of characterization except that of the first-person point of view (the main character telling his own story). His most common device is the Type, a character who is simply a one-dimensional embodiment of a single human trait which is thus isolated and ridiculed. Hungry Joe, for example, simply typifies the slobbering lust of the tormented, immature male; Scheisskopf typifies love of precision parading. Types are not "real," of course, except in this sense: they do represent the way we see certain people who relate to us through only one trait. Another kind of character that Heller uses we may call the Personification of an issue or situation. Major Major Major Major and his enemy, Captain Black, actually personify two political forces, while Milo Minderbinder is "Big Business" incarnate. Many of Heller's characters, the types and personifications especially, are literally identified with a Tag-Name. Dori Duz, for example. The root "Dor" is, in all names, related to gift. And Dori Duz does give. At least a score of names in Catch-22 will repay such attention. Many a figure will prove to be a Symbolic Character: for example, Major de Coverley symbolizes Patriarchal Divinity. Heller uses the Realistic Character for several of his figures: Luciana and the Chaplain are well-developed, three-dimensional persons. The Chaplain especially is explored in depth. And for his main figure Heller uses an Everyman character. Yossarian is sometimes a surrealistic character, sometimes a realistic one but always symbolic and mythopoeic in his proportions.

POINT OF VIEW

Since Heller uses a flexible "point of view" to very great artistic advantage, it may be valuable to review her just what we mean by the whole question of "point of view." Basically, an author can choose to tell his story either subjectively, in the first person (I, we), or objectively, in the third person (he, they). The subjective approach means, of course, that one of the characters narrates the action. Advantage: we can empathize fully with that character, be completely inside one mind. Disadvantage: we can perceive only what the narrating character can perceive at the moment, and only in the way he interprets it! We can see other characters only from the outside. The objective approach means that the author speaks in his own voice as traditional storyteller, able to be anywhere to report any action, physical or psychological, by any character, as he sees fit. If he uses all the prerogatives of the storyteller approach, we say the author is acting as author omniscient: arrogating to himself godlike powers to transcend all barriers, to know all. But he may tend, while using the objective approach, to limit our view mainly to the world of one character, so as to gain some of the advantages of the subjective approach.

Heller will seem, for chapters on end, to be using this limited objective approach. Actually, he never gives up any of his prerogatives as author omniscient. His flexibility adds to the excitement and variety: for several chapters, we center on Yossarian's world; then we may pull back for in-depth historical perspective on another character's life; we may zoom in again to be inside the Chaplain's mind. In this way Heller in effect gains something of the peculiar advantages of each point of view.

ANACHRONISM

Ostensibly, the main action takes place late in the European side of World War II, say roughly 1942–1945. But Heller deliberately uses many **anachronisms** to extend the action and **themes** down to the present. IBM machines as described in *Catch-22*, for example, are post-war developments; Milo Minderbinder delivers a statement that parodies a notorious remark of the 1950s; and the idea of the Chaplain's hiding "secret documents" in a plum tomato is a **satire** on a famous domestic espionage case of the 1950s. We shall note many **anachronisms** in our textual analysis.

FUTURISM

Heller's extension of the situation of *Catch-22* way past World War II results in his being quite prophetic. His treatment of subsidized agriculture, corruption in the medical profession, and psychoanalysis, to mention just a few objects of his scorn, adumbrates the subsidy scandals and the criticism of organized medicine and orthodox psychoanalysis that characterize the 1970s.

LITERARY AND CULTURAL PARALLELS AND ALLUSIONS

Catch-22 is permeated with **allusions** to other literary works, used sometimes to universalize the situation, sometimes to create an ironic contrast, sometimes to effect Heller's mythopoeic purposes. There are, for example, indirect references to the poetry of Gerard Manley Hopkins; Alfred, Lord Tennyson; Shakespeare; Dante; T. S. Eliot, and others. There are also direct **allusions** to the prose of Fyodor Dostoevsky, the poetry of Eliot and Francois Villon, the drama of Shakespeare, and many other literary works. Mythic, religious, and cultural **allusions** are made to ancient Roman rites; the modern Festival of Lights; the Hebraic Garden of Eden, Satan, and Voice in the Wilderness; the Christian Crucifixion and Temptation of Saint Anthony. Historical and political **allusions** abound. The student will find that the textual analysis that follows will provide him with scores of specific examples of this major device.

PROSE STYLE

The vast range of Heller's modes and moods requires a highly flexible prose style. His serious "realistic" scenes he renders in sensuous language, language both textured, rhythmical, and metaphoric. His farcical and satiric scenes he renders in perfectly structured and well-timed sentences and paragraphs. Heller's control is nowhere better illustrated than in his great variety of sentence patterns (**syntax**), his choice of words (**diction**), and his figures of speech (**metaphor**).

SENSE APPEAL

In his descriptions, Heller carefully appeals to all our senses. In Chapter Twenty-Six, for example, he helps us see the bloodstain on Yossarian's uniform and empathize with his horror at the sight: a ... crimson blot ... crawling upward rapidly along his shirt front like an enormous sea monster rising to devour him

To help us get the total sensation of Yossarian's swoon, Heller makes us hear what Yossarian hears:

... a great baritone buzz swallowed him in sound.

To make us feel what Yossarian's sewn-up wound is like, Heller says:

... the stitches on the inside of his thigh bit into his flesh like fine sets of fish teeth.

METAPHOR AND WORDPLAY

Notice that many of these sensuous descriptions are accomplished in terms of metaphors, imaginative comparisons that establish a similarity between dissimilars. Heller is especially bold in his use of similes, or **metaphors** that achieve the comparison with an outright equal sign like like or as. Thus the soldier in white was like an unrolled bandage with a hole in it or like a broken block of stone in a harbor with a crooked zinc pipe jutting out

These **similes** shock us profoundly into understanding that the soldier in White is a thing. But Heller is also adept at **metaphors** in which the comparison is more implied, more subtle:

Yossarian was laid up in the hospital with a burst of clap he had caught on a low-level mission over a Wac in bushes ...

Here the sexual passage in the foliage is compared with the graceful hedge-hopping flight of a plane, and the burst of clap sounds for a moment like, and hence is compared with, a burst of flak. Thus wordplay of all kinds - scores and scores of puns and **similes** and other figures of speech - contribute to the resonating effect of Heller's prose.

GAGS AND SYNTAX

Heller's humor especially requires strong command of sentence structure. Notice that many of the gags achieve their effect because they set up an expectation ...

Colonel Cathcart had courage and never hesitated to volunteer ...

which is then violated with an unexpected substitution or addition:

... (his men) for any target available.

Again:

All over the world, boys were laying down their lives for (what they had been told was) their country.

But other gags depend on word-play enhanced by parallel structure:

The pictures never came out, and Hungry Joe never got in.

Parallelism, indeed, carries much of the message:

They were lovely, satisfying, maddening manifestations of the miraculous, instruments of pleasure, too powerful to be measured, too keen to be endured, and too exquisite to be intended for employment by base unworthy man.

But Heller is masterful in all sentence structures, and in all sentence lengths too: on page 57 (Dell) he runs a fast-paced sentence into well over 100 words, and he ends the chapter (page 60) with a two-sentence paragraph beginning with a two-word sentence followed by a six-word sentence. Such exuberant variety, on every level of language usage, contributes immeasurably to the excitement of the story.

CATCH-22

THEMES

CLASSIC "DROP-OUTS"

In every period of crisis, there emerge in art as in life characters who reject the status quo and take the first lonely and courageous steps toward a better world. Yossarian ranks with the greatest of these, including, in American literature, Huckleberry Finn and Lieutenant Henry. Huck and "Nigger Jim" take a long trip down-river which gives the author, Mark Twain, an opportunity to treat his hero and his reader to a cross-section of society, with its irrational feuds, its hypocrisy, racism, exploitativeness, and narrow greed. Huck, with his simple of love of nature and his capacity for genuine human feeling, can only "drop-out" from a world of such values, and the book closes with his planning to strike out anew. In the same tradition is the hero of Ernest Hemingway's *Farewell to Arms*. An idealist, Henry has volunteered to serve the cause of the Allies in World War I even before his own country becomes involved. After months of combat, of direct observation of human suffering and sacrifice, he finds himself doubting all absolute values. Words like "glory," "honor," and "in vain" cease to have meaning, they embarrass him, they sound obscene.

Disillusioned with the militaristic mind and with the aims of the war, he deserts to neutral Switzerland.

PARALLELS

Parallels in characterization and story among *Catch-22*, *Huckleberry Finn*, and *Farewell to Arms* are important to the student of literature and of American culture. Both Twain, Hemingway, and Heller make it clear that society is the villain and that the only kind of personal heroism left is refusal to play the game. When we say that it is important for Heller's plot that Yossarian takes a long time to make up his mind, we think how important it was for Twain that the Mississippi is a long river: the journey must be long enough to give us a representative cross-section of the depraved society the hero is rejecting. And when we think of Yossarian's entering the war with courage but with no particular illusions, we realize that Yossarian's generation was closer to resistance from the very start than Lieutenant Henry's was; yet there are still just as few places to go! Yossarian feels that except maybe for England, Sweden is the one place left not ruled by "mobs with clubs." But Switzerland was simply a refuge to Lieutenant Henry, a neutral place; while Sweden is not only neutral, it also stands in Yossarian's mind as a place of advanced attitudes and positive human values.

ANTI-HERO OR HERO?

A traditional hero acts the way we should act, according to the values of the Established Culture. An anti-hero then, is one who acts the way we would act if we were not enthusiastic about the Establishment. It is possible, of course, for a New Hero to emerge, one who acts as though he places the values of humanity above the values of the Establishment. Like Antigone, then, Yossarian begins as an anti-hero and develops into a New Hero.

NEW HERO VS. OLD SYSTEM

If we were to try to summarize Yossarian's experience, reactions, and reflections, we might say he finds it impossible to live within the Establishment, even to reform it, because: it tends to treat human beings as mechanisms, to value conformity above creativity, to regard records as more real than people, to indulge in official lying as a matter of smooth policy. The System tends to use war not so much to fight a national enemy as to regulate its own people. It fosters power struggles which victimize the fighting man in wartime and the creative person in peacetime. On every level, the System needs scapegoats and always finds them. The Establishment formulates humanitarian policies not for its own practice but for use in measuring the enemy, for propaganda purposes. Corruption runs rampant in all professions and institutions because private greed is sanctified. Massive, all-inclusive as this indictment may sound, it is actually a mere tight summary of some of the conditions contemplated by Yossarian in *Catch-22*. As Nelson Algren, himself a major novelist, observed, *Catch-22* contains the "strongest repudiation of our civilization, in fiction, to come out of World War II."

YOSSARIAN AS EVERYMAN

Joseph Heller obviously intends us to regard Yossarian as Everyman. First of all, note that we have no physical description to particularize him. Each of us may imagine his appearance as we will! Further, he has no particular background, no detailed history. We know what Nately's mother sounds like, where Daneeka performed illegal abortions, and how Cargill "earned" his living, but we know nothing about how Yossarian came to be what he is. He is called an Assyrian, which means he comes from that part of the world we regard as the Cradle of Civilization. The first part of his name is Assyrian, the second part is Armenian, and the full name sounds an echo of Jesus. His nickname, Yo-Yo, is equally exotic and unspecific. Y-O are the initials of Yossarian and Orr, his tentmate and alter ego; a yo-yo is something that can go with verve only so far before it is pulled back; the name Yo-Yo is given to Yossarian by his new tentmates who know about his relation with Orr; in any event, Yossarian hates the name Yo-Yo and uses it only when he wants to indicate that by accepting the "odious deal," he surrenders his real identity. More significantly, Yossarian describes himself very carefully as Tarzan, Mandrake, Flash Gordon, Bill Shakespeare, Cain, Ulysses, the Flying Dutchman, Lot in Sodom, Deirdre of the Sorrows, Sweeney among the Nightingales, and Supra-man. With the exception of the last, these are all culture heroes who are also outsiders: wanderers, outlaws, artists, drop-outs, people who are both exceptional yet accepted.

JUNGIAN EVERYMAN

Notice another implication in Yossarian's list of personal identifications. The analyst Carl Jung believes that in addition to a personal unconscious, each man possesses a collective unconscious, a total memory of the total experience of the human race. On many counts, then - his unrevealed physical particularities, his unknown history, his careful identification with numerous exceptional people who blend into everyone's experience - Yossarian is to be regarded as Heller's Everyman.

YOSSARIAN AS SUPRA-MAN

But Yossarian also declares himself to be Supra-man, and the careful literate distinction that he makes is typical of this sensitive hero. Superman is simply man writ large, a bigger, stronger, more powerful version of man. The difference between super and supra is the difference between magnitude and quality. Yossarian hopes to surpass man: The man of the Old System described above. Since the Supermen (the "big men" - the Minderbinders, Dreedles, and Scheisskopfs) are satisfied with the Old System, it will take Supramen to create the New.

OTHER CHARACTERS AS REFLECTORS

In addition to showing us how Yossarian reacts to and finally rejects the System and its Supermen, Heller also defines Yossarian in terms of numerous personal relations. Most important of all is Orr, a complementary character. Orr and Yossarian, deep down, have such similar values that they each (privately) have planned and hoped for the same salvation. The differences between them are significant; In the very symbolic act of tent-making, Orr has been the overall director, relating coolly and rationally to their needs. Yossarian has supplied the brawn and the temperament. In discussions of their relation to the war, Orr has been cautious or facetious, keeping his own counsel but planning fantastically well, so well that at last he can offer Yossarian a chance to share the fruit of his plans. Yossarian has been moody and inchoate, protesting but floundering, also keeping his ultimate hope - a neutral country - as secret as fantasy. There we have it. Orr has been the ego, the objective logic; a Yossarian, the id, the subjective imagination. They would have made perfect pair, and Orr knew it.

An analogous relation, one that prefigures the resolution of the Yossarian-Orr partnership, is the one between Yossarian and Luciana. She correctly predicts a phase in his feelings toward her, and once he has hindsight, he wishes he hadn't let her go. Such failure to grasp the essence of the overall situation quickly is Yossarian's greatest weakness. With all his brilliance, sensitivity, and honest emotional struggle, he lacks that same quality that Hamlet lacked: the ability to pull it all together at once, in time.

But see how many good values are represented in Yossarian's reaction to others. Even if it is partly in retrospect, he does admire and appreciate the essence of Luciana and Orr. He tries to protect Clevinger from the follies of his own positivistic approach, Dobbs from his own suicidal extremism, McWatt from his own blind destructiveness. He pities Minderbinder for his narrowness of vision. In relations with women, Yossarian has escaped the very common attitudes represented by Hungry Joe, Aarfy, and Captain Black. In his attitudes toward manhood, he has avoided the common American tendencies to equate cruelty with potence (Havermeyer) or equipment with potence (McWatt). He is the only one in the Group, except the Chaplain, to show the slightest concern for the next generation. Of all the men who know about Kid Sister, Yossarian is the only man trying to help her.

Yossarian's Personality. From the beginning, we are impressed with Yossarian's ability to question **cliches** and shibboleths, to think for himself, yet to value what's great about the past: Villon, for instance, and the Tree in the Garden. He values individuality and freedom more than "status" or official recognition. He keeps money and machinery in their place as means not ends. He is more interested in humanity than in organizations. And when The Organization turns against human values, Yossarian (like the Chaplain) has the courage to remember that there is a Higher Law than the State, that there are times in history when the State is the Villain, when what is needed is a new kind of Hero.

CATCH-22

TEXTUAL ANALYSIS

CHAPTERS 1-5

CHAPTER ONE: THE TEXAN

Title

The opening chapter is named after a character who believes in the power of language and therefore has an extraordinary effect on the combat men he meets in the hospital.

Exposition And Suspense

The early sections of a novel must, by their very nature, be devoted largely to introducing the characters, their situation, and their background. Since **exposition** (as the material in such sections is termed) tends to be static, the author has to counteract this by creating sufficient interest - even suspense - so as to justify our reading further.

Setting

The officers' ward at the base hospital provides a good setting for these purposes. As the attention of the main character, Yossarian, wanders from bed to bed, or is commandeered by doctor or chaplain, we quickly meet a representative number of men in wartime service and sense their situation and attitudes.

Themes Through Characterization

The various attitudes of the hospitalized soldiers seem to indicate that genuine, sustained communication is at a standstill. Men are either withdrawn, or cautious and anarchic in what they say, or speaking volubly and saying nothing. One patient is always "unimpressed." Yossarian does not divulge the real state of his health until he can time such revelation to his advantage. The Chaplain knows the men resent his inquiries about their well-being; he represents religion, traditionally a binding force, but he lacks confidence in his mission.

That communication is regarded as an absurd game is clear from the way Yossarian censors the enlisted men's letters - any pattern of deletions will do the job - and the way he feels free to let others enjoy the pseudonymous names he uses for the censor's signature. But even a game becomes suspect as soon as it takes on meaning: Yossarian gives up chess as soon as it becomes "interesting."

Two characters especially symbolize a breakdown in communications. The Colonel of Communications is extremely ill, obliged to be exclusively with himself. And the Soldier in White, totally bandaged, with his output carefully drained and then fed back into him as intake, obviously symbolizes - among other things - the totally self-contained, totally isolated man. He has come as close as a man can come to being a piece of apparatus, a mere regulated mechanism.

The one person in the ward still possessed of a naive belief in the possibility of sustained verbal communication is the Texan. He does not seem to notice that the other men are turning away from him; he holds "conversations" with the mummified Soldier in White, not at all dismayed that he gets no answers. He talks so much, all the sick men volunteer to return to combat. For these men, facing a barrage of ack-ack is easier than facing a salvo of words. Serious verbal discourse is abominated as deceptive, self-compromising, self-deluding.

Themes Through Wit

Verbal discourse is literally a joke to most of the men. And their wit, as well as the author's constitutes one of the main reasons we read on. Each superb pun or gag makes us hope for another. Because patriotism in America is sentimentally associated with Mom's apple pie, Yossarian calls it matriotism. Heller cannily develops the thumbnail sketch of the Colonel of Communications in a series of brilliant plays on words. He spends all his time getting messages from the Interior (not of Italy, it develops, but of his own body). In appearance he is gorgeous: but not in the usual sense of radiantly colorful! No, he is exquisitely florescent with decay. And the pun on pathology and pathos will warm the heart of any student of etymology. Most of the gags are based on utter reversals of expectation. "Nately had a bad start. He came from a good family." Dunbar is "one of the finest, least dedicated men in the ... world." Such gags not only delight us and surprise us, they introduce other **themes** of *Catch-22*. For example, they emphasize the fact that beliefs so conventional as to be enshrined in **cliches** are for that very reason open to reexamination. Furthermore, all of these puns and gags tell us that life is one long series of discontinuous "bits," of one outrageous contradiction or anti-climax after another.

Structure And Theme

The structure of the chapter adumbrates the structure of the novel. Note that Heller opens with a few interest-arousing remarks about Yossarian and the Chaplain. Then, abruptly the narrative spirals off on a series of free associations, not returning to the Chaplain for four pages. The further we read, the more we realize that the narrative spirals and spirals, and that this shape is closely related to the **themes** of the novel. Each chapter, like Chapter One, is strewn with hints of coming attractions. Since some materialize within the chapter (like the Yossarian-Chaplain situation), we begin to have confidence that all such hints will pan out. For example, we sense that Heller's very first mention of Catch-22 is a non-committal one, that there's more to come. Note that near the end of Chapter One we hear about a cetologist (specialist in whales and other cetaceans) who is shanghaied into the Medical Corps because of a faulty anode in an IBM machine. This brief mention of the absurd consequences of a machine error foreshadows a "major" divulgence that will not occur until 73 pages later. At that time, the earlier event will echo in our memory, lending greater credence to the "major" statement of the motif.

Chapter One, then, suggests a world in which communication has broken down, traditional beliefs are suspect, men are mechanized and organized for absurd and anti-human activities.

CHAPTER TWO: CLEVINGER

Significance Of Chapter Titles

By Chapter Two we realize that the simple title (usually a character's name) that Heller gives to each chapter typifies and signifies. Chapter One was named after the character who typifies belief in the power of language, from which most of the men flee. Chapter Two, it develops, is named after a character who typifies passionate belief in principles that are never examined, the kind of person whom Yossarian pities.

Change Of Setting

Having used the hospital-ward as a suitable setting for introducing us to combat men in various attitudes of indifference, isolation, and malingering, Heller now uses Yossarian's return to duty to introduce us to the world at war. Passage from or to the hospital is significant in *Catch-22*: we learn in Chapter Two that frequent hospitalization is one of Yossarian's techniques of war-resistance; both Chapters Two and Three open with reference to such passage; this passage proves to be a main signal of cyclical developments in the plot.

Characterization Via Tent-Setting

Yossarian's tent is significant because there he lives with Orr: the Yossarian-Orr pairing is one of many significant pairings off among characters. Note that in this pair, Orr is the brain and Yossarian supplies the brawn, which explains why it takes Yossarian the whole book to understand the secret of all of Orr's activity, and why Yossarian ultimately follows Orr's lead. For the moment, it is significant that Orr takes good care of himself: as a matter of fact, he is both a hedonist and a tent-maker, which suggests the master tent-maker in all hedonistic literature: Omar Khayyam (Omar the tent-maker, author of the Rubaiyat, which praises hedonism and rails against the fate that brings all to dust). The faint literary allusion here is reinforced later by reference to "Iranian rice" and by a sudden thick barrage of literary allusions, which makes it clear that Heller intends us to accept this as a major technique of *Catch-22*. Note that Orr and Yossarian share their tent with a "dead man," who will become one of the main symbols of the book and a member of another significant pair: two victims of official record-keeping. Starting with Yossarian's tent, Heller is able to go from tent to tent to introduce more of his characters.

Literary Allusions

Starting in Chapter One with "unspringing rhythms" (a punning reference to the poet Father Gerard Manley Hopkins' technique of "sprung rhythm"), Heller has been using echoes of our previous literary experience to help create the atmosphere he needs. After the suggestive play with "tent-makers," Heller has Yossarian identify himself with numerous literary heroes from Ulysses and Lot down to Deirdre of the Sorrows and Sweeney among the nightingales, and to many culture heroes like Superman and Tarzan. What Heller accomplishes here is to identify Yossarian as Everyman. The technique is similar to Joyce's in *Finnegans Wake*. If, as Carl Jung tells us, every person includes in his *Collective Unconscious* knowledge of all his ancestors, then Yossarian is the cumulative person he declares himself to be. Note too the reference to Sweeney, a character in T. S. Eliot's poetry, which will also serve as a valuable aid to understanding *Catch-22*. Clevinger, who cleverly sees that Yossarian's self-description as Everyman really means "everybody is Jehovah," compares Yossarian to Raskolnikov, a character in Dostoevsky's *Crime and Punishment*: Raskolnikov believes that the superior person is above the law (hence the references here to Superman, for Raskolnikov's beliefs were similar to Nietzsche's concept of the "Ubermensch"). And indeed Yossarian is both Everyman and Superman, because he is proceeding now not according to the Law of the Establishment but according to his Private Law of Survival. However, Yossarian, with his quick sensitivity to the nuances of language, prefers to call himself Supra-man: for super means over or above more in the sense of bigger, more than, whereas supra also implies transcending. A super-man is simply bigger, more powerful, than an ordinary man; but a supra-man has transcended man. Yossarian's form actually is closer to that of Nietzsche, who said, "Man is something that must be surpassed." Yossarian yearns to surpass the absurdity of human activities like war.

Theme Development Via "Gags"

Heller continues to attack these absurdities by breaking apart the **cliches** in which the absurdities are enshrined. Thus, Heller does not simply say that boys were laying down their lives for their country. He shocks us with a simple, unexpected insertion. "... boys were laying down their lives for what they had been told was their country." They have been told so often that it's their country that they believe it without question. But Yossarian questions all cliches, with shocking results, and renders the shock into gags more memorable than the **cliches** they **parody**. For cliches are the "principles" in which Clevinger and Appleby "believe passionately" simply because they do not examine them.

Yossarian Vs. "Democratic Logic"

As a natural extension of his skeptical approach, Yossarian exposes an absurd use of democratic appeal in political reasoning.

"They're trying to kill me," Yossarian told him. "No one's trying to kill you," Clevinger cried. "Then why are they shooting at me?" ... "They're shooting at everyone," Clevinger answered. "They're trying to kill everyone." "And what difference does that make?"

Clevinger does not realize that he has passionately defended two contradictory beliefs, which he has uttered in two successive speeches!

(1) No one is trying to kill Yossarian. (2) They are trying to kill Yossarian.

Clevinger, Heller shows, has been brainwashed into believing that if it's happening to everybody, it's not happening to you. Heller later invites us to see that this tactic effectively reduces protest against mass unemployment, mass slaughter, mass political injustice of any kind.

CHAPTER THREE: HAVERMEYER

Title

This is the third chapter in succession named after a character who represents a human trait that Yossarian dislikes. Havermeyer, a lead bombardier, is a trigger-happy killer who lingers in dangerous situations because he enjoys destruction, even though his lingering also endangers the lives of others. Heller's masterstroke here: when Havermeyer can't kill the human enemy, he fiendishly baits and shoots field mice. He is pointedly contrasted with Yossarian, who had been the lead bombardier but was demoted because he carried "evasive action" too far.

Structure

Heller develops Chapter 3 by spiraling back over situations foreshadowed in Chapter 2, by free-associating to other times and places, and by **foreshadowing** anew: for example, why did that whore give Orr that limited beating, literally "holding her punches" until she knocked him out in a very special way? Also, Heller calmly mentions in passing the night that Milo Minderbinder bombed his own squadron. Every "main" course includes appetizers for the next meal.

Style

The style continues as a constant alternation from staccato "gags" to serious, lofty, highly literary passages, to vernacular and obscenity, back to "purple patches," back to slang and gags, and so on.

Significance Of "Tag" Names

Like other great writers before him, Heller does not hesitate to "tag" his characters with telltale names (think of Shakespeare's lady of easy virtue, Mistress Tearsheet). By the time we first hear mention of ex-PFC Wintergreen in Chapter Three, we realize the importance of appreciating these names as capsule descriptions. Wintergreen, obviously, will be evergreen, through winter as well as summer. "Aarfy," short for "Aardvark" - literally, "earth pig" - is also obviously a dog. General Dreedle is a creepy combination of dread, wheedle, and treacle, a thick, sticky cloyingly sweet syrup. General Peckem obviously enjoys fighting his way up the "pecking order" and, as Heller himself says, "He was a prick." Clevinger is a clever cleaver in close quarters, and just as unsubtle in more subtle atmosphere. Cargill is a common name which, as Heller uses it, suggests a car with gills: indeed Cargill does enjoy such a weird combination of modern and primitive traits on the scale of human evolution. The name Cathcart is less explicit in its suggestiveness. If a catch basin is a cistern that catches matter that won't pass through the sewer, what is a catchcart? Colonel Cathcart is the answer. Milo Minderbinder is a gem. Milo was a Greek and greedy athlete who stopped at nothing; he carried a four-year old cow on his shoulders into the Olympic stadium, slew it with his fist, and ate it, all in one day. Our present Milo is also good at minding everybody's business and at binding up their minds. Orr is a name for us to watch, as the various meanings suggested by the sound emerge in the action: OR, ORE, OAR. And Yossarian himself? His name (according to a comparative literature expert, J. P. Stern) contains an Assyrian stem with an Armenian ending and "an echo of the name of Jesus." Yossarian calls himself an "Assyrian," and later, as we shall see, he feels like Jesus. Note that Yossarian stands out in contrast to a series of Anglo-Saxon or at least "North European" names.

Themes

Heller continues to exemplify his major **theme** of the absurdity and cruelty that characterize a military machine and also introduces a related **theme**: the corruption of other professions in our society. The Military Establishment is characterized in Chapter Three as an organization that cynically changes the rules that people live and hope by: "They were in a race and knew it, because they knew from bitter experience that Colonel Cathcart might raise the number of missions again at any time." (Heller will ultimately invite us to discover the parallels to this "catch," like giving people pay-raises and then inflating the currency.) Thousands of men suffer because of a jurisdictional dispute between generals; they are charged, for example, with responsibility for keeping up the morale of the USO entertainers whose sole reason for coming to a combat area is to keep up the morale of the fighting men. Irrelevant emotional appeals are used without embarrassment: "How would you feel if your own mother traveled over three thousand miles to play the accordion for some troops that didn't want to watch her?" With Colonel Cargill, whose genius for ineptitude proves highly profitable in business (it guarantees a fast tax write-off when one is needed), Heller widens his assault on the unbridled cynicism in American institutions.

CHAPTER FOUR: DOC DANEEKA

Title

Chapter Four is named after a character who typifies, for Heller, the corruption and decadence in American professional life: for Daneeka is a physician not dedicated to the public service.

Another Pairing

Doc Daneeka's corruption is initially indicated by his allowing two ex-mechanics, Gus and Wes, to diagnose and prescribe for men or "sick call." They use assembly line and computer-like (Yes-or-No) techniques. Gus and Wes constitute another pairing of characters (e.g., Generals Dreedle and Peckem; tentmates Orr and Yossarian; two symbolic patients: Soldier-in-White and Colonel in Communications), all of which alerts us to the importance Heller assigns to such balancing and/or polarizing.

Satire On Military Establishment

Heller's ridicule of the military mind continues with: a farcical telephone routine which shows that half a dozen top "brass" have no idea who T.S. Eliot is (by mid-World War II, Eliot was already well established as the leading Anglo-American poet and arbiter of poetic taste); a **satire** on Army "orientation" sessions in which it is revealed that while America's alleged war-aim is to smash Fascism, the American military mentality is itself fascist (also a **theme** of two other World War II novels: Norman Mailer's *The Naked and the Dead* and Kurt Vonnegut's *Slaughterhouse-Five*); and an out-right reference to a military career as the "military business."

Literary Allusions And Punning

Note that Heller keeps us continually reminded of T. S. Eliot, whose relevance becomes clearer: Eliot's *The Waste Land* develops the **theme** of sterility of modern life through the techniques of free association and literary **allusion**. Both Eliot's **theme** and Eliot's techniques figure in *Catch-22*, as will even Eliot's language later in the story. Another allusion in Chapter Four also has long-range implications, since it foreshadows the revelation of details of Snowden's death, a central event in Yossarian's experience and consciousness. At an "orientation" meeting, Yossarian wants to know "Where are the Snowdens of yesteryear?" This brilliant pun alludes to a famous line in a poem by Francois Villon:

Mais ou sont les Neiges d'antan? (But where are the snows of yesteryear?)

In addition to the pun, this **allusion** has many reverberations for Yossarian. Villon was a fifteenth-century dropout, a poet who spent much time as an outlaw, either fighting the police or serving time in jail, but always contemplating imminent death on the gallows.

Characterization

In contrast to the ignominious Doc Daneeka and the uncultured and inept colonels and generals, Yossarian emerges in this chapter as a sensitive, subtle, and brilliant man. Like Hamlet, he feigns eccentricity to cover his withdrawal from a society whose values are anathema to him.

CHAPTER FIVE: CHIEF WHITE HALFOAT

Title

Chapter 5 is named after a character who typifies the **irony** of the anti-fascist war. In World War II, Americans were fighting fascism, theoretically, because the Nazis were racist, genocidal, bent on enslaving and obliterating whole populations in concentration camps in order to create "lebensraum" for deserving fascists. But the presence of Chief White Halfoat in the American Army is an ugly reminder of American sanctimoniousness in this regard.

For the Chief represents the red race who suffered genocidal war, and were herded into prototypal concentration camps, after white racists invaded his country.

Themes

In Five, Heller continues to explore, concurrently, four themes: (1) corruption in American society, begun earlier with thumbnail sketches of business-man Cargill and physician Daneeka; (2) racism in America, introduced in Chapter One when the Texan was nonplussed to hear that maybe the Soldier-in-White might be a "nigger"; (3) the bold sophistry of Establishment rationale; (4) the unspeakable horror of war as represented in the Snowden trauma; Heller also touches, in novel fashion, on (5) modern man's alienation from his own body.

Structure

Note how these diverse elements are unified in the "accidental," ostensibly "episodic" manner that Heller uses throughout. Yossarian - who has flown more missions than are required but is forced to fly more and more as headquarters raises the "limit" - visits Daneeka's tent to ask whether he can be grounded for insanity. Thus he first must hear Doc Daneeka's story of his pre-war career, including examples of unsavory practices and unethical attitudes; then must hear Daneeka's story about two patients, which is a kind of parable; then, since Halfoat is Daneeka's tentmate, Yossarian is also exposed to Halfoat's story about how his tribe was forced to move again and again, because of their genius for locating oil; finally, Yossarian gets to ask Daneeka about being grounded, and learns the best (now classic) example so far of *Catch-22*, which sets Yossarian to free associating from one thing to another until he relives that fatal flight with Snowden - but he cuts the Snowden memory short as it approaches its still undivulged **climax**, leaving us in a state of suspense on this motif.

Another way of looking at Heller's method of plotting as represented in Chapter Five: while one **theme** (Catch-22) reaches its fullest statement, on one level at least, another **theme** (Snowden trauma) is left incomplete, as foreshadowing.

Catch-22

Sophistical, cyclical logic, full of hidden curves and nonsequiturs, has been used in earlier dialogues, notably in Chapter Two where we saw Clevinger blindly entertaining (and passionately expounding) two contradictory premises at once. But by Chapter Five the situation builds up to sophistry so staggering that even Yossarian staggers from it: Daneeka can ground a flyer for insanity; but he would have to ask to be grounded first. Yossarian does ask, and that's his undoing ... "... there's a Catch," Doc Daneeka replied. "Catch-22. Anyone who wants to get out of combat duty isn't really crazy."

The broad symbolic significance of Catch-22 was caught by Robert Brustein, one of the first critics to review the novel:

Catch-22 is the unwritten loophole in every written law which empowers the authorities to revoke your rights whenever it suits their cruel whims; it is, in short, the principle of absolute evil in a malevolent, mechanical, and incompetent world. Because of Catch-22, justice is mocked, the innocent are victimized, and Yossarian's squadron is forced to fly more than double the number of missions prescribed by Air Force code.

Daneeka's Parable

Daneeka's anecdote about two of his patients is a good modern example of a parable, a short narrative from which a moral can be drawn. We are given no direct clue to the "moral," which in itself points to the parable technique; and the prominence of Saint Anthony in Daneeka's recollection of the **episode** reminds us that the parable is a Christian instrument. Notice the suggestiveness and mystery behind the facts: Daneeka examines a young wife to try to ascertain why she is still childless; although she is wearing a Saint Anthony Medal, neither she nor her husband seems to know who Saint Anthony is! Finding her a virgin, Daneeka explains "technique" to the couple, but later the husband returns and attacks the doctor as "a wise guy." Heller allows us to fill in the details as we will, but no matter how we do that, we are ultimately led to see that this is a parable, with the appropriate delayed reactions, about modern man's total alienation from both his animal and his spiritual heritage. Heller's artistry is further manifest in a postscript: after telling the story, Daneeka himself cannot recall having mentioned Saint Anthony. Thus Heller reinforces the idea of the unrelatedness, disconnectedness of our experience.

Poetic Description

As part of his alternation from gags to poetry, humor to "seriousness," Heller composes in Chapter Five one of the most effective narrations of a combat mission to be found in all our war literature. Especially vivid and memorable are Heller's sensuous descriptions of the B-25's on their lumbering take-off, of Yossarian's feelings as he sits in the plexiglass nose of his plane, and of the flak bursting all about him.

CATCH-22

TEXTUAL ANALYSIS

CHAPTERS 6–14

....

CHAPTER SIX: HUNGRY JOE

Title

Six bears the name of a character who illustrates the psychological effect on combat men of arbitrarily changing the rules they live by.

Heller's Psychology

Heller's intensive analysis of Hungry Joe's torments demonstrates the author's ability to draw ingeniously on modern psychology. Joe is revealed as being especially susceptible to arbitrary military cruelty because he is already the victim of a malady rampant in the society that produced him: "hungry" for sex, Joe suffers deep guilt feelings about that hunger. Then, allowed to expect release from combat duty because he has kept his side of the bargain by flying the required number of missions, he is maddened by hunger for his reward and frustrated again every time Colonel Cathcart breaks the bargain by changing the required number. Thus, the Super-Ego (the internalized voice of repressive authority) that made him feel irrationally guilty about his sexual needs is now cruelly reinforced because once again his human hope for human pleasure is punished. One could go so far as to say that if civilian society had not already crippled Joe with this in-built conflict, he would not be so conditioned now to accept the sadistic tyranny of Catch-22.

Catch-22

Significantly, Heller chooses this chapter in which to give the simplest definition of Catch-22, one most easily recognizable to all persons with military experience: the official regulations may "guarantee" a man a certain right, but he must also obey his commanding officer. Hence, if the C.O.'s orders conflict with the rules, as Cathcart's do, the men must still obey them. The extensions into civilian life are numerous: for example, a policeman may be making an illegal arrest in order to break up a demonstration, but the demonstrators must submit to arrest or else they will be "guilty" of disobeying the police! By the time the courts assert the law and free the demonstrators, the police have accomplished their purpose. This is the kind of "loophole" Brustein saw as symbolized in *Catch-22* (see discussion of Chapter Five).

Heller's Irony

Heller's handling of Hungry Joe's torment exemplifies the author's genius for developing ironical situations into surrealistic proportions. The agony of waiting to discover if this time he will actually get his reward is so unbearably great that ultimately Joe prefers combat to his nightmares of guilty hope. "Every time Colonel Cathcart increased the number of missions and returned Hungry Joe to combat duty, the nightmares stopped and Hungry Joe settled down into a normal state of terror with a smile of relief." Here Heller is characterizing the Age of Anxiety. Hungry Joe comes to prefer certain misery to uncertain hope. As in his conditioning to accept repressive sexual mores, he is here conditioned to fear what is good for himself.

CHAPTER SEVEN: MCWATT

Irony In The Title

Chapter Seven is named, ironically, after a character who plays only a peripheral role in the dialogue and free association, which are devoted mainly to Yossarian's liver trouble and Milo's black marketeering. Why does the author virtually snub McWatt in his "own" chapter? The emphasis in the chapter seems to reflect Yossarian's attitude toward McWatt. It seems to be Yossarian who regards McWatt as the "craziest of them all" because "he didn't mind the war." We should recall now that in Chapter Two, McWatt was first sketched as a crazy man who enjoys frightening people by flying low over their tents or their diving rafts. This all suggests that Yossarian pays little attention to McWatt because he is a boy-man. (Note that McWatt doesn't mind the war; Havermeyer revels in it.)

Point Of View

We find ourselves saying that "Yossarian pays little attention to McWatt" because by now we feel that the story is being told mainly from Yossarian's point of view. This raises a critical question of interest to the student of literature. An author has a choice of several points of view. He can identify - and make us identify - exclusively with one character by having that character himself narrate the story in the first person. If *Catch-22* had been told from this (1) subjective, first person point of view, then it might have unfolded something like this:

Usually, my pilot was McWatt, and I think he's the craziest of them all because he doesn't mind the war.

And then we would never know anything that the "I" had not himself been able to perceive or discover. We would be limited to his knowledge, his ignorance, because we would sense everything from inside his skull-case, with all the subjective modifications of outer reality that would imply.

Or the author could take the extreme opposite, the (2) objective point of view. He would stay outside all his characters, as though he were a cameraman recording all events externally, impartially. Of course he would use the third person, talking of his characters as "he," "she," "they."

Or he could modify that third person approach in either of two ways. He could go inside and outside any or all characters at will, telling us, for example, what A secretly thinks of B and how B feels because he doesn't know what A thinks of him. Here the author would simply be reporting all action, mental and physical, in the third person. Since he thus would, for artistic purposes, be arrogating god-like powers to himself, this is called the (2a) author omniscient approach.

The remaining possibility is a compromise, an effort to combine some of the advantages of the objective and subjective approaches. The author describes all characters in the person, from the outside, but is so partial to one character that although we are not inside his skull, we at least feel we are looking over his shoulders. Thus the (2b) limited third-person point of view allows us to watch the hero watching the world without losing our ability to pull back and see him equidistant from the other characters.

It might help to make a further distinction between the two points of view that focus on one character. In the (1) subjective first-person approach, we feel that for artistic purposes at least, author and hero are one. But in the (2b) limited objective third-person approach, we feel that the author and hero are separate but that the distance can be narrowed or widened as the author sees fit for unfolding his tale.

Heller's Point Of View

In the first seven chapters, Heller has used the limited objective approach. Gradually we have come to feel that we are seeing the world mainly as Yossarian experiences it. No other character's impressions are reported so fully, and we learn about other characters mainly as they interact with Yossarian. But we still look at him too from the outside, so much so that the author occasionally allows the image to include facts that Yossarian could not then know. Hereafter we shall note instances of this "pulling back" by which Heller expands our knowledge beyond Yossarian's immediate ken. As we shall see, Heller will sometimes pull all the way back to reassert his rights as author omniscient.

CHAPTER EIGHT: LIEUTENANT SCHEISSKOPF

Title

Eight takes its title from the harshest "tag" name given any character in *Catch-22*. For readers who know German or Yiddish, the "tag" Scheisskopf of course adds to his characterization from the start. But for those who need a translation, Heller withholds it until the revelation will add to the effect. In either case, after seven pages of experience with the man's nature, we are delighted to hear the translation used as an epitome:

> Speculation grew rampant among his closest friends. "I wonder what that Shithead is up to," Lieutenant Engle said.

Themes

The harsh "tag" name is justified, from Heller's standpoint, because in this chapter he delivers one of his bitterest denunciations of militarism and uses Scheisskopf as its paragon. In his concentration on precision parading, Scheisskopf illustrates the militaristic tendency to reduce people to mechanisms. In court-martialing Clevinger for daring to make recommendations for improving cadet morale, Scheisskopf illustrates a militaristic tendency to repress initiative and evaluation and to encourage absolute conformity. In serving at Clevinger's trial as both prosecutor, defense counsel and one of the judges, Scheisskopf serves as a symbol of authoritarian justice.

Heller, Mailer, Homer

Again, Heller treats a war **theme** in common with Mailer. In Mailer's World War II novel, *The Naked and the Dead*, a fascist-minded American general says that an Army has good discipline when every man fears his superiors and holds his subordinates in contempt. The truculence of professional military men has been a **theme** as far back as *The Iliad*: Homer characterizes Achilles as a man so violent in temperament he is unfit for civilian life and even much feared by his fellow soldiers. Heller's conclusion to Chapter Eight - in which Clevinger realizes he will never be hated by the Nazis as much as he is by his own superior officers - is a brilliant extension of this **theme** into our own day.

Characterization Techniques

Scheisskopf is characterized by caricaturization, or extreme exaggeration of certain traits to the exclusion of others irrelevant to the author's aim. The caricature is reinforced by contrast between Scheisskopf and his wife. She is fun-loving, outgoing, open to new experiences; he is grim, single-minded, has lost sight of the ends for the means. Heller also continues to develop Yossarian's character by contrasting him with Clevinger. The two are listening to Scheisskopf's appeal to the men to explain to him "what's wrong."

"I want someone to tell me," Lieutenant Scheisskopf beseeched them all prayerfully. "If any of it is my fault, I want to be told."

"He wants someone to tell him," Clevinger said.

"He wants everyone to keep still, idiot," Yossarian answered.

'Didn't you hear him?" Clevinger argues.

"I heard him," Yossarian replied. "I heard him say very loudly and very distinctly that he wants every one of us to keep our mouths shut if we know what's good for us."

"I won't punish you," Lieutenant Scheisskopf swore.

"He says he won't punish me," said Clevinger.

"He'll castrate you," said Yossarian.

"I swear I won't punish you," said Lieutenant Scheisskopf. "I'll be grateful to the man who tells me the truth."

"He'll hate you," said Yossarian.

Yossarian was right, and Clevinger was court-martialed because he ignored Catch-22. Again, Yossarian is revealed as brilliant, insightful, sensitive. He listens to the tone, motive, quality, the context and the spirit of language, whereas Clevinger listens to its literal meaning only. It will be useful to compare Yossarian's knowledge of communication in Chapter Eight with his conduct in Chapter One.

CHAPTER NINE: MAJOR MAJOR MAJOR MAJOR

Title

The chapter is captioned after a character whose name alone exemplifies Heller's use of the technique of extension ad absurdum. Born with the family name of Major, sired by a father who loved himself so much he could think of no better first for middle name for his son than Major, and promoted from private to Major by an IBM machine, this character is used by Heller in further exploration of several major themes.

Themes

Major's "machine-generated" promotion symbolizes the further mechanization of our lives: Human errors tend to be easier to correct, whereas a machine programmed to recognize "Major" as a rank rather than as a first name is likely to make errors so far-reaching they are irreversible. Three other events in the Major's life combine to make this chapter an important variation on Heller's **theme** of corruption in American institutions: his father's exploitation of Federal subsidy to agriculture (by which he grows richer by not growing alfalfa and hence can buy more land on which not to grow more alfalfa so as to grow richer); young Major's trying so hard to conform that he is hated as a nonconformist (because he carries out Christian ideals literally); and Captain Black's generation of a Grand Loyalty Oath Crusade strictly to embarrass M.M.M.M. (he is given no chance to sign it). These three developments, interwoven in one of the longest chapters in the novel, show that the author sees cynicism, perversion of all decent values, and irresponsible power as characterizing American life. Note that each of these is also a variation of Catch-22. Finally, Heller brings to a crescendo in this chapter his **theme** of the breakdown of communications introduced in Chapter One. Major M. M. Major's gradual withdrawal pulls together several strands of the narrative: he is isolated from his friends by being made commanding officer; he is overwhelmed with superfluous meaningless written communications; he is further alienated from reality by the cynical misuse of loyalty oaths (men about to face death are forced to prove their loyalty by first signing an oath!). Major's "return to the womb" symbolizes the end of communication.

Extension Ad Absurdum

Each of these thematic developments is based on the absurd extension of an existing condition in military or civilian life. For example, some American farmers have "earned" upwards of a million dollars a year from subsidies to agriculture, while the "farm bloc" in Congress has used its power to prevent aid to crippled urban areas.

Point Of View

Chapter Nine illustrates what we said earlier about Heller's flexible use of the objective point of view. While he has tended to limit himself mainly to Yossarian's direct experience, Heller feels free to "pull back" and reassert his rights as detached story-teller. For example, what happens in Major Major's trailer when he is alone can be known only to an author omniscient.

Anachronisms

Heller's deliberate use of **anachronisms** shows that he intended that his **satire** apply to post-World War II life as well. For example, "IBM machines" (in the sense in which Heller satirizes them in Chapter One and Nine) were not yet in use in World War II. "Loyalty oaths" flourished in the Fifties, farm subsidy abuse in the Sixties.

Literary Allusion

Heller begins his portrait of Major M.M. Major by comparing him with "Miniver Cheevy." A rereading of E. A. Robinson's poem will show the student that the parallel extends beyond his being "born too late." For example, Miniver Cheevy carried everything one step further than might be expected: "Miniver thought and thought, and thought..." and then, the unexpected addition: "And thought about it."

CHAPTER TEN: WINTERGREEN

Title

Ex-Pfc (and sometimes ex-Corporal) Wintergreen's name typifies the soldier's determination to survive, like an evergreen shrub, through winter as well as summer.

Themes And Techniques

Wintergreen's being discovered digging and refilling holes (e.g., engaged in the kind of makework so often given soldiers, sailors, and prisoners simply to break their will) is another manifestation of Heller's continual parallel to Eliot. In *The Waste Land*, Eliot's **protagonist** remembers that "Winter kept us warm, covering earth," when life could survive in minimal fashion as "dried tubers." Note too that Wintergreen is virtually the only enlisted man among the "cast of thousands" to be so fully developed or to appear so often. There is **irony** here. In most novels, there are a few officers over many enlisted men, and malingerers are confined usually to the latter. In *Catch-22*, while there are many shirkers, all hanging on for dear survival, they are mainly among the officers with just Wintergreen to show that enlisted men also despise the war! This is one of several chapters in which the "title character" comes in - and is left - by mere free association. Actually the chapter is a series of thumbnail sketches of Appleby, Towser, Dr. Stubbs, and Mudd. The Dead Man in Yossarian's tent - of course, his name is Mudd - is another extension ad absurdum of the **theme** of the irrationality of bureaucracy: Mudd was never able to enter his name on the roster because he was rushed into combat as soon as he arrived and was killed forthwith. Therefore, officially, he never arrived because he never signed in. How much this kind of bureaucratic nonsense really plagues a soldier's life is something that every veteran can document ad nauseam.

CHAPTER ELEVEN: CAPTAIN BLACK

Title

The chapter is titled after the character who, for Heller, typifies the blackest of all villains: the man who proves Dr. Samuel Johnson's point that patriotism is the last refuge of a scoundrel.

Theme And Techniques

Just as efficiency is destroyed at the top by struggles between Generals like Peckem and Dreedle, so - Heller shows - efficiency is weakened in the middle echelons by vicious power struggles between people like Major Major and Captain Black. Disappointed that he has not been appointed C.O., Black launches his "loyalty oath" campaign strictly to cripple Major. Since Black is a staff officer now burdening men with intolerable extra work (signing an oath at every step), Black's action makes it possible for Heller to add this ironical note to his assault on bureaucracy: the people who actually do the fighting are now "dominated by the administrators appointed to serve them." The symbolism of this situation is clear: in many areas in modern life, the actual creator (the engineer, professor, or writer) has to carry an ever-growing hierarchy of empire-building vice presidents, "managers," and third-assistant chiefs.

Deus Ex Machina

Heller uses here the technique of **deus ex machina**. In Greek drama, a complex situation was often resolved by the sudden appearance of a god. In Chapter Eleven, this god is obviously Major de Coverley.

Irony

The kind of snarl that small minds like Captain Black can "create" can be unraveled only by divine interference. Major_____ de Coverley is such a majestic, towering figure that his contempt for the crippling loyalty-oath procedure puts it unquestionably in its place.

CHAPTER TWELVE: BOLOGNA

Title

The first chapter not named after a person, Chapter Twelve is named after a place that becomes a:

Focal Point

Bologna offers Heller a chance to compare, contrast, and further explore his characters by showing how they all relate to one focal point in time and place. Non-combat officers like Cathcart and Black take fiendish delight in the prospect of an American assault on the powerful stronghold of Bologna. As Heller has made clear before, Cathcart always has the courage to volunteer the lives of others. While Cathcart is thinking of his own glory that his men would be gaining for him, Black sadistically enjoys the men's suffering over even the prospect. Significantly, most of the men dread the coming mission as they would a death-warrant. The pre-battle apprehension that Heller creates so beautifully is reminiscent of the tension among soldiers in Shakespeare's *Henry V* and in Kubrick's production, *The Paths of Glory*. Heller again contrasts Clevinger's and Yossarian's attitudes on a crucial issue: Clevinger offers the conventional arguments, redolent of (to adapt Tennyson):

Ours not to reason why, Ours but to do and die

while Yossarian sums it up:

The enemy ... is anybody who's going to get you killed, no matter which side he's on, and that includes Colonel Cathcart.

The power that war gives certain people to send others, arbitrarily, to their death has been a **theme** in literature since ancient times (see the story of David's sending Uriah into combat in order to gain Uriah's wife, Bathsheba: Old Testament, 2 Samuel XI, XII).

| CHAPTER THIRTEEN: MAJOR_____ DE COVERLEY |

| Title |

Thirteen is captioned after the name of a regal character who has already served as **deus ex machina**. His name, and various descriptions of him, are rich in literary allusions.

Cultural Allusions

The name "Major _____ de Coverley" echoes a name famous in English culture. "Sir Roger de Coverley" is, first of all, the name of an English dance, similar to the "Virginia Reel." Then, in the early Eighteenth Century, Joseph Addison created a fictitious character, "Sir Roger de Coverley," a country gentleman supposedly descended from the supposed inventor of the dance. Roger de Coverley was the leading member of a fictitious club which supposedly wrote and published The Spectator, an English periodical actually written by Joseph Addison, Richard Steele, and others. Finally Addison "killed off" de Coverley so that as he said, "nobody else might murder him." And then Joseph Heller resurrected de Coverley for his own literary purposes: note that the Major is always described in mystical and patriarchal if not divine terms. We should recall here that in the scene in which he descended **deus ex machina** to end the Loyalty Oath farce, he was described as "Jehovean" and indeed the men in his way parted before him "like the Red Sea." The lecherous old man who injures Major de Coverley's eye is significantly described as resembling Satan. Also, de Coverley's personal name apparently cannot be uttered: an ancient Hebrew proscription about the name of the Divinity. Still, Major de Coverley's attitude toward World War II is more Greek than Hebraic, indeed, it is distinctly Olympian: he looks down on it as The Spectator would. His main duty is to find apartments in captured cities for the men to use on rest leave: he is more concerned with sexual than martial activity (more with the dance than the parade). Zeus certainly did favor Venus over Mars.

Point Of View

Once again Heller has pulled away from his partiality to Yossarian and gives us a "wide-angle view." Only a novelist reserving to himself the rights of author omniscient could tell us how upset Nazi Intelligence is over the identity of this austere Major.

Themes

Heller continues in Chapter Thirteen to explore his **themes** of the corruption and absurdity of the Military Establishment. Having built de Coverley up as a godlike figure, Heller now contrasts de Coverley with Milo Minderbinder, than whom we can imagine no human more depraved. But Milo corrupts de Coverley too: Zeus can be bribed, especially with savory foods from Malta and Sicily!

In this chapter Yossarian is revealed as involved, willy-nilly, in the cover-up logic used by the military mind. Again Heller shows how Catch-22 pervades Yossarian's life: ordered to destroy the bridge, unable to release his bombs on the first run, he felt he had no alternative but a second run, in which he does destroy the bridge but loses a plane. Who, now, is responsible for the loss, Yossarian who risked a second run (when the enemy antiaircraft enjoyed the advantages of a second try!) or Cathcart who ordered destruction of the bridge? Colonel Korns' solution - "to act boastfully about something we ought to be ashamed of. That's a trick that never seems to fail" - results in Yossarian's decoration and promotion (for bravery in going back!) and of course leaves Yossarian a compromised man.

CHAPTER FOURTEEN: KID SAMPSON

Title

The chapter is named after the pilot who is deliriously happy when Yossarian (who has sabotaged the intercom system) orders the plane to abandon its Bologna mission and return to the base.

Historical Allusion

Kid Sampson calls himself "Admiral," inviting an ironical association with Admiral Sampson of Spanish-American War fame. He was credited with destroying a Spanish squadron, although not actually present at the battle, because it was fought in accordance with his instructions. Indeed, after Kid Sampson, Yossarian, et alia leave their squadron, the other planes do carry out the mission successfully. The parallel is typical of Heller's extraordinary enrichment of his narrative with resonances from history, literature, and politics.

Contrasting Descriptions

Chapter Fourteen contains a lovely description of the beach at Pianosa, intended to serve as extreme contrast to the equally effective description in Chapter Thirteen of the bloody, fiery mess over Ferrara. Both passages show Heller's ability, whenever he is interested in **realism**, to appeal to our senses of sight, sound, touch, and smell. Notice Heller's technique of alternation: Chapter Fifteen will contain another brilliant, harsh description of air - vs. - ground combat.

Symbolic Bathing

Yossarian's solitary and languorous swimming is a gravely symbolic act, a kind of baptism, a ritual of lustration. His act of sabotage in the plane constitutes an important step away from the Establishment.

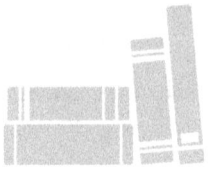

CATCH-22

TEXTUAL ANALYSIS

CHAPTERS 15-24

CHAPTER FIFTEEN: PILTCHARD AND WREN

Title

The chapter is named after two operations officers who are tagged by Heller with mocking names and are described as men to whom war is the best thing that ever happened. As Alfred Kazin has said, "War is still the one 'big' experience that the common man will have in his life." To Piltchard (a pilchard is a common sardine) and to Wren (a common brown bird), life apparently offers no other opportunities for growth or self-expression.

Pairing

Once again, Heller "pairs" off his characters, adding to two C.I.D. men, two generals, two colonels, two medical orderlies, these "joint" operations officers who blandly punish Yossarian for his defection on the first run over Bologna by making him the lead bombardier on the second run.

Contrasts

Heller's technique of alternation of effects is nowhere used more reliably than in Chapters Thirteen-Fourteen-Fifteen. Thirteen was bloody. In Fourteen, the squadron had unexpectedly found Bologna wide open, helpless, with no antiaircraft fire. In Fifteen, they now return nonchalantly to Bologna to discover the city rearmed and powerfully ready. Fourteen had ended with a soft, warm scene of peaceful sky, water, and sand. Fifteen takes us into shattering violence in a sky filled with explosions. Yossarian's men had been "lulled, lured, and trapped."

CHAPTER SIXTEEN: LUCIANA

Title

Sixteen is titled after an Italian girl whose name, like her conduct, suggests light, clarification: she flings open the window of Yossarian's room to let in the sunlight. Such symbolic action is part of the ritual performed by the girl chosen to play "Santa Lucia" in the Festival of Light observed in many European lands (for example, Sweden).

Characterization

This chapter demonstrates Heller's ability to characterize in traditional, realistic, dramatic fashion whenever that suits his purpose. Against an environment that typifies the licentious abandonment of war (reminding us that since Homer, artists have represented the extreme sexual license as one reason why men tolerate if not welcome war), Luciana emerges as a person morally unblighted by the ugly cynicism around her. Her frank but healthy sexuality is contrasted with Aarfy's prudishness and double standards. Of course, even her perspective is twisted by Catch-22, at least on the level where existence must be viewed in terms of language (she feels Yossarian must be crazy to want to marry a non-virgin, and therefore he himself is unmarriageable) but she could not have totally escaped the brainwashing administered by patriarchal society. Note that she correctly predicts Yossarian's elation afterwards at having had a beautiful woman purely for love, and that Yossarian's humanity is revealed when he realizes the shallowness and transitoriness of his own attitudes compared with her dignity and equipoise. The portrait of Luciana is the work of a talented painter.

Contrasts

In addition to using contrasts in characterization, Heller continues to use contrasts in situation, alternating from Ferrara bloodbath to Pianosa swimming to Bologna bloodbath to the sweet Luciana affair in Rome to the ugly interruption by lascivious Hungry Joe.

CHAPTER SEVENTEEN: THE SOLDIER IN WHITE

Title

From the caption we realize we are spiraling back to the time period covered in Chapter One when we first met the Soldier-in-White and when, actually, he died. For the still living, he remains as the man who was an Unknown Soldier even before his death.

Themes And Techniques

Both the state of the Soldier-in-White and the treatment accorded him reinforce Heller's message about the **dehumanization** of man. In two of his best similes, Heller sees the Soldier-in-White as resembling "... an unrolled bandage with a hole in it" or a "broken block of stone in a harbor with a crooked zinc pipe jutting out." The way nurses Duckett and Cramer take pride in polishing the apparatus controlling the Soldier's intake and output suggests again that man himself has been reduced to a piece of equipment. They are so efficient in their concern with means, they seem to have forgotten the ends. The artillery captain sums it up perfectly when he suggests they "hook the jars up to each other and eliminate the middleman.... What do they need him for? The mummified soldier is the focal symbol in everyone's consciousness as the characters contemplate mortality, venereal disease, the relationship between conduct and fate, the trap of sex. Heller's remorseless assault on corruption continues through his characterization of Daneeka, to whom professional ethics means never giving testimony against another doctor. We are reminded again of the importance in Heller of pairing and tags. Duckett is suggestive not only of ducat and "duck-it," but also, via thieves' **rhyme**, of a stronger term. And Cramer, with all her conscientious fussing and stuffing, does seem like one who crams.

CHAPTER EIGHTEEN: THE SOLDIER WHO SAW EVERYTHING TWICE

Title

While it does refer to a man whose fatal illness is revealed by this name, the title is also a strong reminder of the techniques and **themes** of *Catch-22*.

Techniques

Spiraling back still further, seeing more with each spiral, we return again to Yossarian's period of training in the States, when he was either enjoying sex with Mrs. Scheisskopf or learning how to stimulate symptoms likely to keep him hospitalized. Handling a discussion of God between two supposed atheists (Mrs. Scheisskopf and Yossarian), Heller gives us a good example of vituperation, or sustained, bitter, verbal abuse. Yossarian's censure of God is so personal and comprehensive it becomes clear that in spite of himself, he does believe in God: but as a malevolent, anti-human force. The **irony** is poignantly compounded when Mrs. Scheisskopf weeps because the God that she does not believe in is a benevolent God Obviously Yossarian's Hell is right here on earth. Having been exposed by one doctor for lying about his "liver symptoms," Yossarian is forced to reenact the dying moments of the Soldier Who Saw-Everything-Twice for the sake of his family who arrived too late for the real death. Heller is working here on several levels at once: satirizing hypocritical, sacrosanct tableaux, like the traditional family-at-the-deathbed scene; forcing Yossarian, like Odysseus, Aeneas, and Dante, to live the Descent Into Hell before doing it for real; **foreshadowing** a more symbolic version of the Descent that will come in Chapter Thirty-Nine. Yossarian, as Everyman, as the Collective Unconscious, will see Everything More Than Twice.

CHAPTER NINETEEN: COLONEL CATHCART

Title

For eighteen chapters, Heller has created suspense by often referring to Cathcart without giving us any in-depth study of him. Now the heading of Chapter Nineteen promises some long-awaited insights into the nature of the arch-villain (who, for his own advancement, arbitrarily and illegally doubles the prescribed number of times each man will risk his life).

Characterization

First through intensive **exposition**, then through dramatization, Heller makes of Cathcart an epitome of hypocrisy, contradiction, and inner conflict. For example, while serving as a leader in an Army fighting for democracy against fascism, Cathcart is revealed as himself pro-fascist and anti-democratic. Heller's gag techniques are at their best in service of this revelation. As we have seen, Heller often takes a familiar **cliche** and gives it several twists. Note how he makes Cathcart echo vulgar anti-Semitic, anti-Negro views but in class terms that show that really Cathcart has no friends at all: "Some of my ... best friends are enlisted men, ... but that's about as close as I care to let them come.... Chaplain, you wouldn't want your sister to marry an enlisted man...." The Chaplain, whose performance in Chapter One has helped prepare us for Chapter Nineteen, finds the one way to prevent Cathcart's coarse plan from coming to fruition. Hoping to be written up in a national magazine, Cathcart proposes prayers before each mission. The Chaplain's feeling that God would not want the enlisted men to be excluded from this benefit kills the idea. Like all persons insecure in their alleged superiority, Cathcart is afraid to extend any benefits to his alleged "inferiors."

Heller makes it clear that anxiety permeates the consciousness of people like Cathcart. He is not an arch-villain through personal volition so much as through the contradictory demands of the system he serves. He is expected, on the one hand, to compete and get ahead; on the other hand, to conform. In order to "get ahead," then, he must, ironically, show little initiative, and always find out what is expected of him. Colonel Cathcart is a victim of Catch-22. All his actions are self-negating. He has no Self. His one great "original" idea - publicity in a magazine over pre-flight prayers - is based on the fact that that very magazine has already run an article about a colonel whose chaplain already does that!

CHAPTER TWENTY: CORPORAL WHITCOMB

Title

The name of an enlisted man, in a novel mainly about officers, stirs interest for the same reason here as it did in the appearances of ex-PFC Wintergreen. Literally, Whitcomb's name means white comb, probably in the sense of the crest on the head of a fowl. Note how Whitcomb does strut in and out like the cock of the walk.

Themes And Situations

Chapter Twenty illustrates again how an authoritarian system thrives on insecurity, truculence, and petty rivalries. In short, it fosters the worst traits in man and stultifies the best. Corporal Whitcomb has no intrinsic interest in his job as chaplain's assistant (personally, he is an atheist) but it is his one vehicle for self-assertion, for "getting ahead." We already feel some affinity between Whitcomb and Cathcart (both have cynical plans for exploiting the deaths of others). Notice too the sinister alliances fostered in the authoritarian system: because of Yossarian's mischievous signing of other people's names to Yossarian-censored letters, the Chaplain has become the focus of a slapstick man-hunt. Of course, the C.I.D. man would exploit Whitcomb's envy of the Chaplain, further poisoning another human relationship in the name of "fact-finding" and in the cause of "justice."

Techniques

The poetic passage in which the Chaplain thinks about paramnesia (the strange mental state in which we feel we have experienced present circumstances on some previous occasion) is another excellent paradigm of the basic plan of the book. Heller's techniques so far have included **foreshadowing** and spiraling back. Notice again the use of **anachronisms** to make the novel not only a World War II book but a post-war book in nature!. The Chaplain's carrying a plum tomato of course means he is hiding secret documents in it! The famous case to which this must be an **allusion** occurred in the Fifties, when some notorious papers were allegedly hidden in a pumpkin. Anachronisms, foreshadowings, free-associations that spiral back in time, all these techniques are intended to foster in us an experience of artistic paramnesia.

CHAPTER TWENTY-ONE: GENERAL DREEDLE

Title

The caption promises to shift the spotlight to the man at the top of the pyramid. Our interest is heightened by various hints that his status is rather like that of the boy temporarily "king of the hill" in the quick turnover game of that name.

Structural Links

Twenty-One is the third consecutive chapter devoted to the anxiety that haunts men in an authoritarian set up. In Nineteen, the Chaplain appealed to Cathcart on behalf of the men suffering from increased combat duties, but especially on Yossarian's behalf. Then in Twenty, the Chaplain went away to brood over his misery, deepened by harassment from his power-mad assistant. Again, Yossarian figured in both the conversation and the meditation. And in Twenty-One, Yossarian is the immediate cause of Cathcart's taking anxious inventory of his reasons for feeling insecure (black eyes) and reasons for feeling secure (feathers in one's cap). In addition to furthering the characterization of Cathcart, the list he compiles serves also to summarize events so far (Ferrara, Bologna) and to introduce some we have not yet heard much about (Avignon).

Themes

In addition to further burlesquing the power struggles among colonels and generals, Heller extends his attack on corruption into the legal profession. A lawyer in civilian life, Colonel Korn represents that kind of legal talent devoted to breaking the law with impunity; using Cathcart as accomplice and dupe, he exploits the chaos of war to engage in currency speculation and black market operations. Meanwhile, the fighting men themselves yearn to return to peaceful pursuits, as is made clear in two symbolic actions in this chapter.

Dream Symbolism

The presence of General Dreedle's nurse at the briefing for Avignon results in a spontaneous moaning among the men. Of course, the General takes his nurse everywhere with him to flaunt his power and privilege. Yossarian and the others respond on the level of pure human and esthetic need. After the mission over Avignon, at both Snowden's funeral and at the formation for decorations (at which Yossarian is to receive a medal), Yossarian appears naked. Dreedle interprets this on one symbolic level - he sends his nurse out of sight. Yossarian intends it, apparently, on another level as well: since Snowden's death, he simply refuses to wear the uniform, especially on official occasions. This symbolic act was prefigured in Yossarian's baptismal swimming on the Pianosa beach after his defection from the first Bologna mission. Both the moaning and the primeval nudity have the intensity of dream symbolism.

CHAPTER TWENTY-TWO: MILO THE MAYOR

Title

The caption is pure bait, promising as it does a story of how Milo extends his power.

Structure

Heller continues to use alternation of mood and technique as one of his main structural devices. After the grotesque briefing session that was turned into a "moaning" session, Heller resumes the realistic vein of the Snowden flashbacks, adding more detail to the tragedy over Avignon, but still shying away from conclusion of that **episode**. Then Heller swings back again giving us two more self-contained satirical situations.

Satire

As we have seen, the name of **satire** is reserved for that literary approach that employs humor, wit, and **irony** to expose and ridicule vices and follies. The two satirical situations in Chapter Twenty-Two are perfect examples of this approach. Dobbs wants Yossarian's concurrence in a plot to assassinate Cathcart: but as Dobbs elaborates on his plan, he extends it "logically" to include Korn, and then, step by step, other "villains" including a friend of Yossarian's but excluding one of Dobbs'! Dobbs is caught in another version of Catch-22. Thus means become the ends, extreme measures become a travesty of their own aims. Dobbs would of course wind up being a super-Cathcart, more arbitrary than the Cathcart he so justifiably hates. In the final situation, Yossarian and Orr go with Milo supposedly on one of his military supply purchasing trips, which turns out to be an inspection of his spreading private empire: from Gibraltar to Istanbul! In each city, he has been "elected" mayor or Shah or viceroy because he has stimulated trade and made at least the middlemen prosperous. But his life is hectic, frantic, and strictly economic in its focus. The more he gains, the harder he has to fight to keep it. By contrast, Orr and Yossarian are interested in people, details of the places, atmosphere; and in spite of the discomfort of traveling with the single-minded Milo, the tentmates enjoy an occasional laugh. "Satire," said Ezra Pound, "reminds one that certain things are not worthwhile."

Characterization

While characterizing Milo and Dobbs satirically - that is to say, holding their follies up to scorn - this chapter also advances the characterization of Yossarian. We see him as above the vices of Milo and the weakness of Dobbs, as refusing to arrogate to himself the right to execute even an arch-villain like Cathcart. Also, we see Yossarian and Orr as a pair, as comrades in the same human pursuits, an important relationship for us to keep in mind.

CHAPTER TWENTY-THREE: NATELY'S OLD MAN

Title And Themes

The caption sums up the **irony** of one of the most ironical chapters, a chapter which in turn gives new symbolic and mythic expression to many major **themes** of the novel. To start with, the name Nately is poignantly appropriate to both the character and the themes: natal relates to one's birth (nativity) and to buttocks (nates). Nately's mother, we learn, places great faith in his genealogy, and he obviously has been a neatly, nattily groomed young aristocrat. However, he knows very little about his real origins, as Chapter Twenty-Three shows. When Nately meets the Old Man (whom we have already identified with Satan) in the brothel, he is unable to account for the fact that this lecherous old cynic keeps reminding him of his own father. For his own father, as he recalls him, is a paragon of propriety, a pillar of aristocratic strength and responsibility. Now Heller deftly gives us a flashback to mother, father, and son, from which we can infer that young Nately has understandably idealized the pater. To us, there is nothing basically incompatible with the suave family man of young Nately's experience and the more candid Old Man in Rome. Young Nately is looking at his real father without his social and family disguise. No wonder young Nately is so unassertive in his relations with the whore facetiously called "Nately's whore." He is relating to her in the presence of a double father-figure, one who is contradictorily both in Super-Ego (conscience) and his Id (instinct): at once both his Good Angel and his Evil Angel!

The Old Man, surrounded by the naked women, is of course also Proteus, the Old Man of the Sea of ancient mythology, and the women are his sea-cows, seals, or mermaids. The Old Man's adaptability alone would tell us this: pro-fascist under the fascists, pro-democratic now that the Americans have arrived, the lecherous Old Man is protean! He is capable of myriad superficial and illusory changes because deep down he is always the changeless essence of change. His age (107) gives him the right to be above wars, dogmas, nationalities, for living that long in Italy he has seen that all such categories and criteria are vain and ephemeral. He knows everything because he is smart enough to believe in nothing trivial.

Ironic Echoes

The Proteus scene in *Catch-22*, like its counterpart in Joyce's *Ulysses* and in Homer's *Odyssey*, reverberates with echoes and **foreshadowings** of the rest of the work. To mention one example: before this scene, the Chaplain has brooded over paramnesia (Chapter Twenty) - later, the Chaplain is to ask Yossarian (Chapter Twenty-Five) "Have you ever ... been in a situation which you feel you had been in before, even though you knew you were experiencing it for the first time?" Ironically, Nately had never seen the Old Man before the war:

yet he had. The **irony** is everywhere portentous: Americans have never seen defeat, but they are the modern Romans, and Rome fell.

CHAPTER TWENTY-FOUR: MILO

Title

As we have seen, Milo was a famous Greek athlete, notable for both his stamina and his physical greed (see p. 19).

Literary Allusions

The opening paragraph is highly wrought with literary **allusions** that develop both the themes, characterization, and techniques. When T.S. Eliot opens *The Waste Land* with the shocking announcement that April is the "cruelest month," he means that the month of renewal can be viewed only with mixed feelings by a sterile, dying culture. When Heller opens a chapter with the observation that April had been the "best month of all" for Milo, Heller further invites us to see that Milo is really thriving on the decay of the culture. And when Heller reminds us that lilacs bloom in April, he is alluding now not only to Eliot's second line but to Whitman's *When Lilacs Last in the Dooryard Bloom'd*, an **elegy** on the death of a hero: Abraham Lincoln. For in Chapter Twenty-Four, Yossarian mourns the death of a hero: Snowden. The **allusions** ramify in many directions by the time we come to Heller's line: "In April a livelier iris gleamed upon the burnished dove." The student may find it profitable to follow through on some of them by way of appreciating Heller's methods. For example, the iris is a perennial flower, but it is also the diaphragm in the center of the eye, and by extension, a type of diaphragm used on the moving picture camera, and it is that iridescent play of colors we call the rainbow. That his gleam should be on a burnished dove suggests that life has become totally artificial, but of course it also refers to the type of furniture found in the lady's dressing room in *The Waste Land.* extraordinary opening concludes with an **allusion** to Tennyson who thought that in Spring a "young man's fancy turns to thoughts of love." Tennyson did not know Milo, whose fancy turns to whatever product is the season's money-maker. This reinforces the contrast we have noted, in Chapter Twenty-Two, between Milo's fancies and those of healthy young men.

Biblical Allusions

The contrast between Milo and more human creatures is further developed in the funeral scene. While Snowden is being buried, Yossarian is sitting naked in a tree. We already referred to Yossarian's nakedness (refusal to wear his uniform) as a return to primal innocence. In describing his tree to Milo, he quotes verbatim from Genesis, calling it "the tree of life ... and of knowledge of good and evil." Of course, Milo insists it's only a chestnut tree. He ought to know. He sells chestnuts!

Other Themes

Milo's values however, are more representative than Yossarian's. Milo's international black-market connections have naturally brought him into contact with the enemy. One of the many "deals" that ensue is that Milo's men should bomb and strafe their own air base. "Decent people everywhere were affronted, and Milo was all washed up until he opened his books to the public and disclosed the profit he had made." As history proves ad nauseam, in our society anything that makes a monetary profit for some selfish schemer is sacrosanct, no matter how ghastly the human and natural loss.

Extension Ad Absurdum

Milo's bombing of his own troops is the best example of Heller's use of the satiric technique of extending an existent condition to show its ultimate implications. Black market operations obviously weaken the army that the operators belong to; they poison the morale of both the troops and the people in the occupied country; they enrich a few soldiers who are using the military position for private profit, and exploit honest soldiers who are dedicated to the war effort. Milo's operations. Heller's famous scene tells us, are the exact equivalent of direct military aid to the enemy.

Cinematic Techniques

The opening pages of Twenty-Four also contain an excellent illustration of Heller's use of cinematic cuts. To show the extent of Milo's operations, Heller cuts rapidly from a B-26 commander in Sardinia, to a B-25 commander in Corsica, to a fighter-plane commander up north, all of them talking to Milo. What seem like three dialogues are actually continuous. For example, Milo mentions breaded cutlets to the first commander and gets his answer from the second; a similar transition links the second and third scenes. In using cinematic techniques in a literary medium, Heller is again following the example of T.S. Eliot but also paralleling the works of closer contemporaries like William Burroughs.

CATCH-22

TEXTUAL ANALYSIS

CHAPTERS 25-39

CHAPTER TWENTY-FIVE: THE CHAPLAIN

Title

We are promised a closer study of a man we have come to sympathize with because of his opposition to the cynical plans of Colonel Cathcart and Corporal Whitcomb.

Themes

The action dramatizes again the breakdown in communications, the isolation of the individual, but the Chaplain's meditations suggest that some millennial change is at hand. When the self-ostracized Major Major and the pariah Chaplain go seeking each other on foot, we have the hope at last of some real breakthrough toward human understanding. But each avoids the one person on the path ahead, not aware in either case that that person is the object of his trip. Their twice passing each other this way, their each missing the other in his quarters and on the road, is a poignant failure of the most serious reaching-out from one man to another so far attempted. The meeting between the Chaplain and Yossarian when the bombardier asks help in getting grounded, is another failure, for the Chaplain cannot help and Yossarian denies the existence of deja vu or paramnesia. (as we have discussed earlier, paramnesia is the feeling that one has been through a situation before, even though one "knows" it is the first such experience.)

Religious Associations

The Chaplain's meditations on deja vu are developed in intensely religious terms, allowing Heller to use some of the basic mythopoeic materials of the Old and New Testaments. During Snowden's funeral, the Chaplain had a vision of a naked man in a tree - actually, of two men, the second clothed somewhat sinisterly and offering the naked one a "brown goblet." The reader, who knows that those two were really Yossarian and Milo, also knows that the object offered was really a ball of chocolate-covered cotton, and that Yossarian himself on that occasion alluded to the Tree in the Garden. But what does the vision mean to Chaplain Tappman? We are left to imagine. Does his own recollection of it suggest Satan tempting man? Or a naked man crucified and a bystander reaching out to give him a sponge soaked in wine? The name Yossarian, we have noted, has vague echoes, in Assyrian, of "Jesus." And in Chapter Thirty-Nine, we shall see that on at least one occasion, Yossarian says he feels like Christ.

There are other apocalyptic signs. Leaving the road-bed to avoid the approaching figure (Major), the Chaplain takes to the woods and meets the terrified Captain Flume, hiding out from the wrath of Chief Halfoat. Captain Flume, prophesies that he will be able to return "When winter comes," by which time he hopes Halfoat will be dead of pneumonia. Notice here the emphasis on change of seasons, and on death as a beginning of a new cycle, both of them **themes** in *The Waste Land*. Notice too the concept of the voice in the wilderness which is of great prophetic importance in both the Hebrew and Christian Bibles. In Isaiah (40: 3-5), the Lord God announces that "warfare is ended," and then a voice cries out in the wilderness, bidding the people (as was the custom when kings progressed through the country) to straighten and level the road. Later, John the Baptist, Hebrew prophet who foretold the coming of one greater than himself, called himself the voice of one crying in the wilderness (Mark 1: 3, John 1: 23).

The withdrawal of each man into himself, the vision in the tree, the voice in the wilderness, the failure to take the straight road - no wonder the Chaplain feels he is receiving signs of a great coming event! But he also feels that he took part in a similar event in a great spiritual crisis in history. Is he, in his guilt-feelings over being of no help to Yossarian, comparing himself with Pontius Pilate? Certainly with somebody in similar circumstances!

Characterization

Through this meditation, the Chaplain reveals himself as one willing to risk insanity in order to achieve insight. Heller's descriptions of this mental state show that he anticipated the contemporary emphasis on the sanity of insanity. Meanwhile, Cathcart too has undergone profound character development. We find him speaking like Whitcomb! One interview with the Chaplain's assistant, and Cathcart has absorbed Whitcomb's ideas and expressions as his own. Now that he has a new form-letter to go to "nearest of kin" of casualties, he needs some casualties and so volunteers his squadron for another attack on Avignon.

Heller's Prophecies

Cathcart's welcoming casualties to try out Whitcomb's letter seemed fantastically vicious when Catch-22 first appeared in 1961. But during the Vietnam War, Bernard Weinraub of the *New York Times* wrote:

> At a briefing ... a brigadier general said with a smile:
>
> "Well I'm happy to say that the Army's casualties finally caught up with the Marines last week."
>
> There was a gasp. A civilian ... said incredulously:
>
> "You don't mean you're happy."
>
> The general was adamant. "Well the Army should be doing their job too," he said.
>
> Jim Pringle ... whispered: "My God, this is straight out of *Catch-22*."

As Heller and written in a novel of the Absurd, the professional military leader needs and welcomes casualties as proof he's functioning.

CHAPTER TWENTY-SIX: AARFY

Title

Aardvark, whose name literally means "earth-pig" and whose nickname sounds like a child's pet name for a dog, is one of Yossarian's pet hates.

Characterization

Heller characterizes Aarfy as a classic case of naive sadism. In the pursuit of women, in the heat of combat, Aarfy's main activity is to gape at other people's emotions. The only reaction that he himself has is to disparage the feelings of others, which of course he must do in order to deny his dependence on them. In Chapter Twenty-Five, Aarfy obviously enjoys Nately's anguish in love and Yossarian's helplessness when wounded. Serving as lead bombardier, Aarfy constantly gets the squadron lost, probably because he is paying more attention to the passionate preoccupation of the men around than to his own duties. The characterization as sadist is borne out by Aarfy's naive expectations that he can plan to control the feelings of others too.

Heller's Sense Appeal

In this combat scene, as in all of them, Heller uses many descriptive words and figures of speech that succeed because they appeal to our senses. To help us both visualize the bloodstain on Yossarian's uniform and appreciate his horror at the sight, the author calls it a "crimson blot ... crawling upward rapidly along his shirt front like an enormous sea monster rising to devour him." To help us get the total sensation of Yossarian's passing out: "a great baritone buzz swallowed him in sound." To help us feel Yossarian's sewn-up wound: "the stitches on the inside of his thigh bit into his flesh like fine sets of fish teeth ..." Notice that all these appeals to our senses (sight, sound, touch) have been accomplished in imaginative comparisons called similes. A good simile creates a shock of recognition of similarity between dissimilars. Heller is author of some forty or more superb **similes** in *Catch-22*, as well as of good examples of other figures of speech.

CHAPTER TWENTY-SEVEN: NURSE DUCKETT

Title

In our analysis of Heller's use of tag names, we commented on the suggestiveness of Nurse Duckett's name. This chapter demonstrates the literalness of her name. It is her ability to "duck it" that precipitates Yossarian's "psychoanalysis."

Themes And Characterization

Here Heller continues his **satire** on the pretentiousness and contradictoriness of the medical profession. Major Sanderson, the psychiatrist, has obviously become a psychoanalyst through studying his own uncured neuroses; he is so insecure that he accuses others of being mad in order to assert his own power and superiority. Heller is especially successful in burlesquing that part of orthodox Freudian dogma that blames maladjustment to society on the individual, as though society itself could never be wrong. Thus Yossarian is "immature" because he has no respect for excessive authority or obsolete traditions; he has an aversion to war; and hates bigots, bullies, snobs, and hypocrites.

Heller's Futurism

Again, Heller anticipated a later development in psychoanalytic thinking. During the 1960s, analysts like Rollo May and R. D. Laing pointed out that society itself can be mad, and that to "adjust" to a mad society is no sign of health.

Symbolism

Heller ridicules psychoanalysis on its own grounds by basing the psychiatric session on Yossarian's alleged dream of fish. The fish is a classic symbol - in literature and religion - of fertility, and the analogy between fishing and loving women is a favorite **theme** in art. (Again, consider *The Waste Land*.) But the psychiatrist feels triumphant to discover the connection in Yossarian's mind, a connection Yossarian is healthy enough to take for granted. Yossarian's ability to manipulate poor Sanderson through the fish symbolism illustrates another point that writers like Heller and Mailer have raised: what happens when the patient is smarter than the analyst (especially if the analyst believes the patient should adjust)?

Tag Names

This chapter adds another to a long list of tag names in *Catch-22*. The doctor who contemptuously sends Yossarian to the psychiatrist (holding them both in contempt!) is named Ferredge, which means iron-edge. Heller exploits the well-known contempt for psychoanalysts among traditional physicians like Ferredge, but of course Heller sees the folly in both their positions: Psychoanalysis could be a fruitful tool in developing man's potential, if it did not so tend to define sanity as conformity.

CHAPTER TWENTY-EIGHT: DOBBS

Title

We are promised more on the character who symbolizes the men's murderous hatred of Cathcart (because Dobbs does contemplate assassination of the C.O.). But from experience, we are prepared also for the possibility that the character the chapter is named after will serve mainly as a launching pad for free association to other characters.

Irony As A Theme

Developments in this and the preceding chapter demonstrate the importance in **satire** of **irony**, or exploitation of reversal. In Twenty-Seven, when Yossarian finally got himself declared insane by an insane psychiatrist, Yossarian still didn't get sent home because the mad doctor filed the insanity report under the wrong name. (Hence A. Fortiori was discharged. Notice the **irony** in the tag name: a fortiori reasoning makes use of conclusions inferred from, and taken to be even more conclusive than, another reasoned conclusion or fact!) Now in Chapter Twenty-Eight, ironies proliferate to the extent that **irony** becomes not only a technique but a **theme**: originally, Yossarian refused to countenance Dobbs' plot to kill Cathcart. Now that Yossarian has changed his mind, it is Dobbs who is opposed to the idea! Here the ironic reversal involves an exact shift in roles. These two ironic developments, completed in two chapters, now prepare us for a greater **irony** which is not consummated until Chapter Forty-Two.

Characterization

Orr has obviously been practicing how to make perfect "emergency" landings and how to survive in a raft at sea. He now urges Yossarian, repeatedly, to ask to be assigned to Orr's plane. Although Yossarian himself has often talked of escaping to a neutral country where he would be interned for the duration, he does not see the connection. Ironically, he passes up Orr's plea and in Orr's next crash, Orr "disappears" alone. In retrospect, Orr looks like a much more generous, warm-hearted character than we had imagined.

Puns And Anachronisms As Theme

Twenty-Eight contains good examples of two more of Heller's techniques. Orr has practiced how to use the little oar that survival rafts are outfitted with. As Orr drifts away from his crew, it's obvious he has taken the alternative in the dilemma Yossarian also faces: either/or. And in one of the crash landings, the men find that Milo, for black-market purposes, has removed the carbon-dioxide cylinders that make it possible for the life-jackets to inflate. He has left a note: "What's good for M & M Enterprises is good for the country." This is an obvious **allusion** to an infamous remark, made after the war allegedly by a Big

Business man serving in the President's Cabinet: "What's good for General Motors is good for the country." Once again, Heller extends an apparently World War II story up into the present, and again, he attacks the corruption in American institutions.

CHAPTER TWENTY-NINE: PECKEM

Title

The name that has earlier suggested the pecking order (among other things) now promises that the story will return to the **theme** of the power-struggle among top commanders.

Themes

But Heller structures his fiction contrapuntally, and so Twenty-Nine actually advances several **themes** at once: not only (1) the empire-building of rival commanders, but also (2) the worsening of communications and (3) the indiscriminate cruelty of war. Notice how the first **theme** ramifies: Colonel Scheisskopf's arrival overseas is welcomed because (a) Peckem can pose Scheisskopf against Cargill in the endless "divide and conquer" routine of oppressive authority; (b) Peckem now can build a new pyramid under Scheisskopf, thereby increasing Peckem's own power; (c) he now has one more colonel to use in his fight against General Dreedle, his acknowledged wartime "target." The communications muddle is complicated by Peckem's use not of the most direct and accurate word but of the most impressive "literary" word. The decision to bomb an entire, undefended village so as to block a road, demonstrates again that in war, military means subvert political ends.

Characterization By Allusion

General Peckem's comparing himself with Fortinbras, a character in *Hamlet* (who stays outside the central action, until everybody has killed everybody else off, and then comes in and takes over) is brilliant and ironic. For it is doubtful that Fortinbras actually planned it that way, while it is not to be doubted that Peckem plans it just that way.

CHAPTER THIRTY: DUNBAR

Title And Theme

Named after Dunbar because of his refusal to drop his bombs on civilians as ordered (he dumped them further up the road: a military target), this chapter explores the **theme** of how war fosters wanton disregard of life.

Structure By Contrast

Again, Heller demonstrates mastery of structure. For purposes of contrast, he divides the action into three segments. The first gives us another instance of McWatt's passion for terrifying people (inside the plane and outside) by flying low. Ironically, Yossarian is made to feel guilty for his dislike of such "pranks." In the second segment, Heller develops a tenderly genuine affair between Yossarian and Nurse Duckett. The first two sections, then, contrast two attitudes: one that nurtures, cherishes, respects life; another that is irresponsible and sadistic. The third section returns to the wanton indifference: buzzing over the beach, McWatt slices Kid Sampson in half at the waist. Dramatic alternation, from indifference to care to indifference, structures one of the best chapters in the novel.

Characterization

McWatt's suicide after his lethal prank adds to the tragedy but softens our judgment of him. The people who cherished life (like Dunbar, Yossarian, and the Chaplain) move further away from people contemptuous of life (like Cathcart, Aarfy, Havermeyer).

CHAPTER THIRTY-ONE: MRS. DANEEKA

Title

We are promised a rare look at civilian life back home.

Themes

Heller renews his **satire** on exploitation of war for personal advantage and on the inhumanity of bureaucracy. Daneeka registered his name on various flight rosters so that he would collect flight pay; but he stayed safely on the ground. Since he had been listed as aboard McWatt's plane and did not parachute out, he is now listed as dead. His protests avail him nothing: it is logically "impossible" for him to be alive. His pay stops, and death benefits go out to his wife. She is better able to ignore her husband's letters "explaining everything" after Whitcomb's form letter and several large insurance checks convince her of the reality of her widowhood. Aside from the **satire** on the quick adjustment that war-widows can make, and the ironic "comeuppance" administered to greedy Doc, the emphasis is on the mechanical nature of bureaucracy.

Pairings And Symbolism

The system has now created two situations that prove that records are more real than people. Mudd was killed in the air but since he had not signed in first, he officially did not go aloft and officially is alive, somewhere; Daneeka signed up but didn't go, and since the plane crashed, he is officially dead. Mudd and Daneeka symbolize the Death-in-Life and the Life-in-Death that bureaucracy can create.

CHAPTER THIRTY-TWO: YO-YO'S ROOMIES

Title And Situation

By the simple plot development of having four young replacements moved into Yossarian's tent, Heller is able to impress on us the "quick aging process" of war. Only twenty-eight, only seven years older than the new officers, Yossarian feels that his combat experience has put a whole generation between him and them. The nickname they give the "old man" (Yo-Yo) and the fact that they think of themselves not as his tentmates but his "roomies" emphasizes the difference between their "collegiate" enthusiasm for, and his mature disenchantment with, the war. Again, Heller achieves his effects through contrasts.

CHAPTER THIRTY-THREE: NATELY'S WHORE

Title

The chapter heading promises more "comic" relief in Rome but the title turns out to have an unexpected meaning.

Social Satire

Chapter Thirty-Three is one of Heller's best demonstrations of ability to raise situation comedy to the level of social **satire**. On the "plot level" this is a farcical rescue of Nately's whore from some high-ranking officers who will not let her go home. But on the satirical level, it is a rollicking spoof first of the pomposity of a certain type of military mind, and secondly of the proprietary pretensions of patriarchal man.

Note that the colonels look - and feel - stupid without their uniforms on; it seems to be not the man himself but the regalia of rank that makes each of them a "commander." Note too that one of them contemplates sexual assault in overt military terms, a la Beauvoir. Again Heller uses contrast effectively: when Nately's whore's rescuers throw the captors' uniforms out the window, the generals, calm emphasizes the colonel's panic.

The romantic **satire** is equally well conceived: all it takes Nately's whore to realize she really loves him is one night's good sleep! Then Heller exploits for all it's worth the difficulties ahead for a "free" woman who falls in love with a male supremacist: he gives her his protection (from other male supremacists) and she gives up her freedom.

CHAPTER THIRTY-FOUR: THANKSGIVING

Title

The most ironical chapter so far begins with an ironical caption. First of all, the men actually have little to be thankful for, decimated, demoralized, desperate as they are. More significant, though, is the fact that the word "Thanksgiving," as used in modern America, denotes a bland, "civilized" version of the wild agricultural festivals of ancient Italy. And in the course of their war-time Thanksgiving Day, the 256th lives history in reverse, starting with the American dinner and reverting swiftly to the Roman festival in which even slaves were permitted to kick over the traces for a day.

Clues To The Parallel

Heller gives us the first clue to this descent into the earthy origins of Thanksgiving cranberry-sauce when he describes the soldiers' drunken celebration as a "guzzling saturnalia" that spreads through the woods and up the hills. Such a description could apply to the revels in ancient Rome, where the temple of Saturn stood at the foot of one of the seven hills over which the saturnalia would spread.

Then Heller symbolizes the descent into history when Yossarian dreams he is racing down an endless staircase: Yossarian is awakened from this dream to discover that the enlisted men are firing machine guns! The orange tracer-bullets serve two purposes: the slaves are kicking over the traces, and they are lighting the candles of the Saturnalia. Since the Roman custom of candle-lighting has become the Christian custom of lighting Christmas-trees, we are reminded now that Milo's lavish handing out of cheap black-market booze is a travesty on both ancient saturnalian and modern customs of gift-giving. The parallels in such festivals, the loss of the sense of "time," are both indicated as the men shout "Happy New Year!"

Our pagan-like New Year's Eve celebrations are closer in spirit to the ancient saturnalia than our puritanical Thanksgiving Day could ever be.

Saturnalian Reversal

In the "Mardi Gras" spirit of the Saturnalia, the world is turned upside down: everything goes. Good and Evil, law and license, ego and libido, appearance and reality become totally confused. People cannot afterward distinguish between what happened and what they phantasied. Going into the saturnalia and coming out of it, of course, provide various degrees of these mixed sensations. Chapter Thirty-Four is developed entirely according to these patterns.

Notice that the Chaplain tells his first lie and loves it; the medical doctors wear guns, armed M.P.s serve as medical orderlies; Nurse Duckett recovers from her "romantic" feelings about Yossarian and reverts to a "realistic" approach: she decides to marry a doctor for his money. Old masks are ripped off, new masks put on. Total remasking is symbolized in the sudden reappearance of a Soldier-in-White. Is he the same one, or another? Given his anonymity, it makes no difference. But notice the sinister suggestion that the Soldier-in-White is really some kind of spying device: is it a recording apparatus, to which, around which, people have talked freely? Or is a live spy listening inside all those bandages? That he is taken away - after his reappearance causes a riot - not by medical orderlies but by the M.P.'s suggests that this time at least, the Soldier-in-White is a plant and (the pun is inevitable) a bugged one at that.

The phantasmagoric and the actual both persist into the return to "normality." Yossarian hit Nately during what seemed like a nightmare; but the morning after, Nately's nose is really broken. Dunbar was really there and helped investigate the machine-gunning during the most unreal state of the saturnalia; but after the return to reality, Dunbar is sinisterly non-existent.

CHAPTER THIRTY-FIVE: MILO THE MILITANT

Title

Just as Milo The Mayor suggested that Milo had extended his economic powers into the political scene, so this caption suggests that this black-marketing officer might at last be doing something soldierly.

Themes

Heller continues his bitter **satire** on capitalist economics, according to which everything is "objectively" controlled by "laws of supply and demand" and people have complete freedom of choice (to pay high prices or starve).

Contrast

Again, Heller uses vivid contrasts to drive home his points. While Milo is arranging to have the men fly extra combat missions under Milo's name. Dobbs and Nately plunge to a fiery death in a battle over La Spezia.

CHAPTER THIRTY-SIX: THE CELLAR

Title

Again Heller uses **irony** in a caption. The title indicates both the basement to which the cynical C.I.D. men take the Chaplain for the worst kind of Stalinist grilling, and the bottommost stage of morale, to which the Chaplain drops because of the successive shocks of Nately's death and the illegal cross-examination.

Contrasts And Echoes

The dishonest, anti-human grilling that the Chaplain is subjected to is contrasted with the honest, sacred grief he has just suffered for the twelve dead men, including personal friends. The spurious interrogation is also an echo of the "trial" of Clevinger.

Characterization

The Chaplain learns anew that there is a higher morality than the State: when the State turns immoral, he feels justified in refusing to identify Yossarian's handwriting, even though he recognizes it as such.

Anachronism

Again Heller extends *Catch-22* into the postwar World. The investigator who says "I have here in my hand ..." is intended to suggest Senator McCarthy, who, during the Fifties, would tell reporters that the paper in his hand (which he never allowed anyone to see) contained lists of hundreds of Communists high in the Government.

CHAPTER THIRTY-SEVEN: GENERAL SCHEISSKOPF

Title, Theme, Symbolism

The very title shocks us, meaning as it does that the ugly power struggle has pushed the most cowardly and irrelevant man of all to the very top. And the divulgence in the scene that follows - that this is a consequence of a miscarriage of Peckem's plot - climaxes Heller's attack on the absurdities of bureaucracy.

The final symbolism, of course, inheres in the new general's first command: everyone will parade. Scheisskopf's compulsive passion for parading has, throughout the novel, symbolized mad emphasis on means instead of on ends. Parading is a part of basic training that helps soldiers develop a sense of solidarity and group efficiency which they must learn to apply to the real and advanced problems of warfare. Fixated as he is in that early stage of military development, Scheisskopf is totally divorced from reality. Furthermore, a non-combatant by principle, personality, and preference, he is totally incapable of the kind of sympathy and justice that Yossarian, Dunbar, and other survivors need.

CHAPTER THIRTY-EIGHT: KID SISTER

Title

The caption reminds us that while some men are conspiring against each other for the right to decide who will die next, and while some men are trying to extricate themselves from the war, the younger generation has been largely neglected.

Characterization And Symbolism

Nately's whore's reaction to the news of Nately's death is an extension ad absurdum of three real factors in the situation. As the bringer of bad news, Yossarian is likely to be abominated in the first place: if Yossarian had not yet arrived, neither would news of Nately's death. But Nately's whore had already heard of the broken nose he had suffered at Yossarian's hands, and in her eyes, Yossarian has contributed toward the destruction of her lover. Finally, Yossarian is part of warmaking manhood, and it is logical for women to blame all men for the death of any man in a man-made war. Again Yossarian is characterized as Everyman. Indeed, he becomes something of a culture hero in this chapter, or, more accurately, a class hero. On his return to the base, he is approached surreptitiously by many who identify with his refusal to fly any more missions. He becomes here a popular outlaw, a Robin Hood perhaps, but then we remember the earlier **allusions** to Francois Villon, the greatest of all popular outlaws. Finally, Yossarian's characterization as Everyman, more concerned with survival of people than with preservation of the Establishment, is perfected in his going A.W.O.L. to rescue Nately's whore's kid sister, who of course symbolizes the future of the human race.

CHAPTER THIRTY-NINE: THE ETERNAL CITY

Title

Heller's heading this chapter with one of the epithets of the city of Rome is both ironic and symbolic. Rome was the center of the ancient world, home of the saturnalia, of Aeneas, of the greatest military and engineering genius of its day (explaining why Americans are often called the Romans of our day). Rome is also the center of the Roman Catholic World, therefore identified with Christian mysteries and verities, Dante, and the Renaissance. Yossarian's turning to Rome, after his quasi-desertion from the Army, is part of his journey as Everyman is search of the Self.

Theme

When the M.P.s are able to destroy the Old Man's brothel and evict all the girls (including the "kid sister") simply because "Catch-22 says they have a right to do anything we can't stop them from doing," then Catch-22 is finally revealed as Heller's name for that sordid principle: might makes right.

Symbolism Of Old Man's Death

Since the cynical Old Man had boasted that his adaptability to all conditions (including Nazism) made him virtually immortal, his inability to survive the M.P.s' raid is further evidence of the enormity of the present situation.

Epic Crisis

Heller evidently intends us to feel that Yossarian has reached a crisis in his fight with the Establishment. Having refused to fly any more combat missions, having gone A.W.O.L., he cannot avoid arrest much longer; his efforts to rescue the "kid sister" have been frustrated; he is up against Catch-22 in its most undistinguished form. What should his next move be? We have a clue in Yossarian's brief recollection of the Old Man, whom we have seen as functioning, on the one hand, as Proteus, Old Man of the Sea, and on the other, as Satan. Both **connotations** are relevant again. Note that in *The Odyssey*, when Odysseus reaches an impasse, he is advised to visit the Underworld. And in Vergil's *Aeneid*, Dante's *Divine Comedy*, and countless other works, when the hero reaches the dead center of life's hurricane, he makes a similar descent into Hell. The journey gives him new knowledge, new insights that enable him to return to his struggle and to prevail.

Yossarian's Descent Into Hell

The place where Yossarian enters the Underworld has been identified by Minna Doskow (in her brilliant paper, "The Night Journey in *Catch-22*") as the "bottom of a hill in a dark tomblike street," outside the police station. "The pervasive gloom through which Yossarian travels resembles Dante's City of Dis or Homer's City of Perpetual Mist in its absence of penetrating light," Doskow points out. Just as Odysseus hears shrieks and wails, and sees only grey specters of once living people; just as Dante sees enacted all about him the cruelty of man to man, so Yossarian hears cries of children being whipped, please of women being molested by soldiers, screams of civilians being clubbed by policemen; at murkily lighted corners he sees the scars of war and poverty on every face. The final horror in his Night Journey occurs, of course, in his scene with Aarfy - who has raped and murdered an Italian girl - when the M.P.'s interrupt to arrest ... Yossarian for being A.W.O.L.

CATCH-22

CHARACTERIZATION

What does Yossarian learn from his Night Journey? More than at any other time, Yossarian gets outside himself and sees that human suffering is universal. In his passionate identification with all of mankind, he feels at one point like Christ, which reminds us of the Chaplain's vision; like Christ, and like the Chaplain, Yossarian has had new evidence that in times of social chaos, the Authorities themselves can be Evil Incarnate. But the full effect of the Night Journey can only be seen in Yossarian's subsequent behavior. Will the universality of cruelty convince him of its inevitability, forcing him to yield to the Cathcarts and Korns? Or will the prevalence of suffering rather suggest that he is even more justified in Resistance? Most heroes - even **epic** heroes - act it out, veering toward one solution, then toward another.

CHAPTER FORTY: CATCH-22

Title, Theme

Promised another corollary to *Catch-22*, we learn the most important one of all for idealists like Yossarian: you cannot compromise with oppressive Authority without losing your identity.

Echoic Structure

Notice that in its structure and even in some of its details, this chapter resembles an earlier scene (see p. 34) in which Yossarian accepted promotion and a medal to help cover up an allegedly "embarrassing" situation. Once again Heller has created in us a strong sense of deja vu.

Irony

But this time around the consequences are greater, and much more ironical; no matter how he decides, he is up against a truly classical dilemma. Acceptance of the deal means return home (but as a "cooperative" hero who plays the game and destroys his own ideals); refusal means court-martial (of course, on unbeatable trumped-up charges). The **irony** is multi-faceted and all pervasive. For example: apparently the colonels want to "buy off" Yossarian alone, offering this special "out" to him only; apparently Yossarian's bitterness that he has fought this battle with no overt support from his buddies is one of the reasons he accepts this private "deal"; yet to the reader, if not to Yossarian (who has been away too much to know), it seems clear the colonels are making the offer only because Yossarian's tireless one-man rebellion has finally sparked mass discontent among the fliers.

Artistic Aims

Thematically, the purpose of this major confrontation seems to be to show us the consequences of compromise with the

Establishment and to prepare us for the inevitability of the real resolution still to come. For the alternatives discussed with Korn and Cathcart are those that obtain only if Yossarian resolves his problem within the System: court-martial or reward for capitulation. But if it develops that Yossarian cannot live with either of these alternatives, then he will have to resolve his situation outside the System. Structurally, the function of Yossarian's tentative acceptance is that it increases the suspense.

Symbolism

Heller uses symbolism to emphasize the fact that abiding by this "deal" will mean a total loss of identity for Yossarian: he tells them to call him Yo-Yo, a name he hates. Notice that a yo-yo can go only so far before it is pulled back!

CHAPTER FORTY-ONE: SNOWDEN

Title

With all the **themes** rising to a crescendo, we expect from the caption that at last we will hear the full story of Snowden's death and its traumatic effect on Yossarian.

Symbolism

Two psychic events - the first of which is communicated to us only on the symbolic level - combine to give Yossarian the insight and strength to resolve his dilemma. (1) Notice that in coming out of anaesthesia, he must again make the passage from phantasmagoria to reality that he made during the saturnalia. This time the fantasy is of a demon who says, "We've got your pal." Now what "they" have got, of course, is part of Yossarian himself: the decent part. In making the deal with the colonels, he surrendered his conscience. He completed the Descent into Hell where (like Dante) he touched Satan. And like Dante, having looked into the face of ultimate Evil, he can still ascend out of Hell, he can still rescue his "pal," which is to say, his soul. (2) This interpretation is reinforced by his free association to the death of Snowden. The terrible secret that Snowden spilled out over the plane (as Kid Sampson was sprayed all over the beach), is simply:

The spirit gone, man is garbage

Thus Yossarian's dream and free association combine to tell him that once "they" have his soul, he will feel like pure garbage. Significantly, it is to the Chaplain, whom we have come to respect because of his courage and self-honesty, that Yossarian first divulges his intention not to go through with the deal: i.e., not leave his soul in Hell.

Structure

Thus the novel comes round full spiral to the opening scene in which Yossarian and the Chaplain first met. The difference, though, is that this time they are real friends, partly because during the interval each has found the "pal" inside himself with which one can make friends outside oneself.

CHAPTER FORTY-TWO: YOSSARIAN

Title

The caption suggests that now we shall meet the real Yossarian, the man who has been through difficult rites of initiation and has made the choices that determine character.

Characterization

Significantly, for the crucial dialogue - the one in which the inevitability of Yossarian's desertion is demonstrated - Heller chooses Danby as the man with whom Yossarian argues it out. For Danby is a liberal, a man who believes in the anti-fascist war, and who has made all the necessary pragmatic adjustments: for example, he cooperates with the Cathcarts because of the "larger issues." Nevertheless, his final concession - that if he also had Yossarian's courage, he could no longer, at this stage of the war, make so many compromises - closes the question of the ethics involved. Notice the contrasts in character development: As Yossarian's choices force him into a more radical position, Wintergreen's and Cathcart's choices force them into a more fascist position as they join hands with Milo to "clean up" before the war ends and to consolidate their power for the post-war world.

Deus Ex Machina

It is a mistake to see the Chaplain's news of Orr's desertion to Sweden as a **deus ex machina** element in the resolution of the story. Yossarian's own departure is a foregone conclusion. News of Orr simply answers the question, departure for where?

Yossarian's intention all along to try to save the "kid sister" would have routed him through Rome in any event.

Symbolism

Again, the "kid sister" symbolizes the younger generation that the Establishment has totally ignored and that only the "dropout" is concerned with. Nately's whore, still trying for the fatal wound, symbolizes the continual danger Yossarian will be in from the "mixed up" scapegoat hunters of the older generation. Sweden symbolizes the neutral country for Yossarian as Switzerland did for Lieutenant Henry in Hemingway's *Farewell to Arms*. Finally, we are reminded of the symbolism in Orr's name and action: he represents the alternative way.

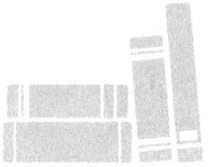

CATCH-22

CHARACTER ANALYSIS

Aardvark, "Aarfy"

A bombardier. His name literally means "earth-pig," his nickname is the one children often give to a pet dog, and he is one of Yossarian's pet antagonists. In the pursuit of women in the heat of combat, Aarfy's main activity is to grin at other people's expression of feelings. He feeds, for example, on Nately's anguish in love and on Yossarian's helpless agony when wounded. Whenever Aarfy serves as lead bombardier, he gets the squadron lost, probably because he is paying more attention to other men's passionate preoccupations than to his own duties. The only real feeling he expresses of his own is his strong disparagement of the feelings of others, which is his way of denying his dependence on them. Significantly, he is no more capable of self-love than of love of others: when everyone else is in swimsuits, Aarfy remains fully dressed, as though he cannot love even his own appearance. In short, Heller presents Aarfy as a type of naive sadist: we say "a type" because the factors that shaped Aarfy's personality are not revealed to us.

Appleby

Air Corps officer. An All-American boy, he is perfect in small matters (ping-pong, craps) because he is undisturbed by big questions (religious, social, political), for which he unthinkingly accepts the prescribed answers. He serves as a simplified version of Clevinger, an extreme foil for Yossarian's intelligence which reexamines all common beliefs as a matter of course.

Black, Captain

Intelligence officer. His name indicates that Heller agrees with Dr. Samuel Johnson who (in his Dictionary) defined patriotism as the "last refuge of a scoundrel." This blackest of all the petty villains in *Catch-22* is one of Heller's anachronisms, for he is modeled on many political figures of the post-war world who launched "loyalty oath" crusades to embarrass and discredit their political opponents. Since his own work is non-combat, he has plenty of time to engage in power struggles and to enjoy the discomfort of those whose job is combat. Note Heller's emphasis, through Black, Aardvark, and many others, on various ways in which war fosters the sadistic aspects of man's nature.

Cathcart, Colonel

For almost half the novel, we know Cathcart only through the effect he has on the other characters. Then, in a series of close-ups and confrontations. Heller reveals to us the inner dynamics of Cathcart's psyche, from which we conclude that he is a hideous product of a society that puts a premium on conformity.

From the beginning, Colonel Cathcart is the arch-villain because, for his own advancement, he treacherously doubles the prescribed number of times each flier must risk his life. We say treacherously because a kind of contract has been made with the combat men: it is understood that after they fly X number of missions, they may be "rotated: to non-combat duties. Cathcart constantly raises the value of X to the point where, for example, Hungry Joe goes nearly insane, Dobbs broods over plans to assassinate Cathcart, and Yossarian simply defines Cathcart as "the enemy," that is, "anybody who's going to get you killed, no matter which side he's on."

Observed at close quarters, Cathcart proves to be an epitome of hypocrisy, contradiction, and inner conflict. While serving as a leader in a democratic war against fascism, he is revealed as himself pro-fascist and anti-democratic. But he is not an arch-villain through personal preference so much as through the paradoxical demands of the system he serves. He is expected, on the one hand, to conform, and on the other, to prove himself in competition, to "get ahead." Ironically, then, he must always find out what is expected of him before he dares show any initiative! Some of Heller's best precisely balanced statements are designed to explain this man:

He was someone in the know who was always ... striving ... to find out what was going on.

He was complacent and insecure, daring in the administrative stratagems he employed to bring himself to the attention of his superiors and craven in his concern that his schemes might all backfire.

All his actions are self-negating. He has no self. In his darkest hour he makes lists of his merits and his demerits not according to some personal system of honest self-evaluation, but according to what other people expect. His one "original" idea - to get magazine publicity by having his chaplain recite prayers before each mission - is based on the fact that the magazine has already run an article about a colonel whose chaplain already does that! He is the constant victim of anyone with higher rank or stronger sense of self: he changes his mind whenever he finds that the General disagrees with him; he is used by Colonel Korn as a "front"; and he takes over wholesale the ideas and even the language of a self-seeking chaplain's corporal who does have a new way to get publicity and who also dislikes the chaplain. Cathcart, like Corporal Whitcomb, illustrates how an authoritarian system thrives on insecurity, truculence and petty rivalries.

Max F. Schulz

He has described Cathcart as trapped in the "day-to-day fret of the social conformist." Heller's portrait of Cathcart reminds Schulz of Coleridge's description of an anxiety-ridden society as one in which one must always be rising as a condition of not falling.

Cargill, Colonel in Special Services

An extreme type who serves two of Heller's purposes: to satirize American business tactics and to expose the absurdity of military logic. In civilian life, Cargill was "known as a dependable man for a fast tax write off' because he could "run the most prosperous enterprise into the ground." This was not easy, what with Government helping business in every possible way! Apparently Heller sees this kind of circular activity as perfectly preparing Cargill for military life. For example, U.S.O. troupes are sent overseas to entertain the men and thus raise their morale. The men are understandably reluctant to have even their entertainment prescribed and regulated. Therefore Colonel Cargill is sent out to force the men to "enjoy" U.S.O. programs in order to raise the morale of the entertainers! Thus Cargill demonstrates Heller's point that in a huge authoritarian system like an Army, keeping up appearances is a major activity.

Chaplain; Captain Tappman; Group Chaplain

A major character, the Chaplain is to be compared with Yossarian in two ways. Like Yossarian, he grows in the course of the action. But unlike Yossarian, he has a pre-war history which gives us greater insight into his struggles. In this sense, then, the Chaplain is the most thoroughly developed character in the book. In circumstances in which interpersonal communication is at a standstill, the Chaplain makes heroic efforts to reach other people, to give some broad human meaning to his own life. In the opening scene, he is painfully conscious of the men's resentment of his efforts to improve their morale. By the final scenes, he has several close friendships and is the man to whom Yossarian first confides his intention not to go through with the "odious deal."

Heller very sympathetically and ingeniously develops the Chaplain's meditations through universal religious symbolism. Reacting to his vision of a naked man in a tree, and to his own sensation that Captain Flume is a "voice in the wilderness," the Chaplain feels he is receiving portents of a great spiritual crisis. He feels he is playing a role in a situation that has been enacted in earlier history. The premonition proves correct and ironical. The Chaplain himself becomes a "religious scapegoat. Although he recognizes Yossarian's handwriting in the censor's note and "signature," he refuses to expose Yossarian even to save himself. In concealing literal truth from government agents who would use it for inhuman and irrelevant ends, the Chaplain rediscovers an ancient religious truth: conscience is a Higher Law than the State's law. It is in this higher sense that he becomes a Christ-figure who takes on himself the "sins" of others.

Clevinger, An Air Corps officer

An educated but naive idealist, Clevinger serves as a foil for Yossarian in three illuminating discussions. By having Clevinger earnestly defend commonly held positions, Heller is able to show how original, flexible, and basic Yossarian can be in his thinking. By having Clevinger take language at its face value, Heller is able to demonstrate Yossarian's broader perception and sensitivity.

Colonel of Communications

A feeble and doomed man, obliged to be concerned only with his own decay, he symbolizes the collapse of communication.

de Coverly, Major

His very name perfectly illustrates Heller's technique of compacting literary allusions, archetypal symbolism, and surrealistic effects all into one intense creation. Why is de Coverley's first name never used in print or speech? Associations crowd in on us. First of all, the ancient Hebrews felt constrained never to utter the name of God! And the Major acts like and is regarded as a godlike power. When he ends the farce of Captain Black's "loyalty crusade," he is "Jehovean" in his serenity, indeed the men before him "part like the Red Sea." In this apparently hopeless situation, _____de Coverley serves as **deus ex machina** (the "god in the machine" who descended on the Greek stage to resolve an impasse). And the Old Man who dares injure de Coverley's eye is pointedly identified as Satanic. Near the end of the war, the major disappears, indicating that God is Dead.

Furthermore, the need to fill in the blank in the Major's name reminds us of Sir Roger de Coverley, an illustrious name in English cultural history. The "Sir Roger de Coverley" was a popular English dance (similar to the "Virginia Reel") for generations before Joseph Addison, in the early 1700s, created a fictitious character by that name who claimed descent from the inventor of the dance. Sir Roger was the leading member of a fictitious Club which supposedly published The Spectator, famous English periodical actually written by Addison, Richard Steele, and other literati. The "Sir Roger de Coverley Papers," as "his" contributions to The Spectator were called, comprise one of the finest series of essays in English literature. Joseph Addison finally killed off Sir Roger so that, as he explained, "nobody else might murder him." But another Joseph resurrects him by way of demonstrating the immortality of mythic figures.

For Heller, the name has additional values. In the Air Force, Roger is the code word for the letter R which indicates that the speaker has received and understood the message and agrees. In other words, to Yossarian and the other fliers, Roger is an utterly necessary and inevitable term of affirmation! But in English slang, it has always been that: to roger a woman has meant, in vulgar speech, to have sexual intercourse with her!

Now all the **allusions** begin to add up! For it's Major Roger de Coverley's main duty to rent apartments for the men so that on their rest-leaves they may have a place in which to enjoy sex! This, of course, is more the Hellenic than the Hebraic side of de Coverley's godlike nature: the **deus ex machina** is a pagan conception. Just as he resolves the "loyalty oath" impasse, so does he solve the men's problems on leave. We are reminded too that a dance-whether called Sir Roger de Coverley or the jitterbug - is basically sexual in nature. Major _____ de Coverley, then, is a theosophic combination of Zeus and Jehovah who guarantees to the men that the basic forms of affirmation shall be theirs. His disappearance is one of the deepest notes of despair sounded in *Catch-22*.

Danby, Major, Group operations officer

He is essential to Heller in the ideological resolution of the story. For Danby is a university professor, a thinker, a liberal who believes in the anti-fascist war, in short, a man able to marshal the best arguments against Yossarian's desertion. Furthermore, Danby has demonstrated his own ability to act on his principles: we recall that he has suffered humiliation at the hands of military authority without losing his faith in the justice of the war. When Yossarian's plans are tested against such rigorous opposition, and when Danby finally concedes that in Yossarian's situation these arguments lose their meaning, we feel the novelist has satisfactorily explored the ethical aspects of Yossarian's "dropping out."

Daneeka, "Doc"

The Group medical officer serves many purposes for Heller: "Doc" typifies the corruption and cynicism in American professional life; he is chosen as the character best able to put *Catch-22* into its most memorable form; his strange "come-uppance" illustrates again (like Mudd) that to a bureaucracy, records are more real than people, and means more important than ends. Note that "Doc" sees medicine not as a public service but as a means of self-enrichment, and that his hypochondria symbolizes this exclusive concern for himself. Note too that the "Parable of the Married Virgin," which illustrates man's alienation from both his physical and spiritual self, is understood by "Doc" only on the level of a dirty joke. That "Doc's" scheming for getting flight-pay without flying should result in his being classified dead while still alive is typical of Heller's **irony** at its best.

Daneeka, Mrs.

She exemplifies for Heller the way many civilians exploit wartime chaos for private gain. Given the official notices of her husband's "death" and her husband's letters explaining the error, she prefers to believe the former because they bring big checks. This kind of punishment for "Doc" - purely "poetic justice" - is the only kind of justice discernible in Yossarian's world.

Dobbs, Air Corps officer

Dobbs' career exemplifies Heller's technique of swinging from (1) extreme humor to (2) extreme horror. (1) In two farcical scenes, Dobbs first plans to assassinate Cathcart for always the raising number of missions, then abandons such plans when he thinks he himself has "made it." Then (2), forced to fly one more extra illegal mission, he plunges to his death. His story tells us that a man may base his principles on what is best for him at the moment and still outfox himself.

Dreedle, General

Although Heller uses Dreedle to illustrate some common abuses of military power, he also makes him a more sympathetic character than the other generals. True, Dreedle flaunts his power to have a consort even at the front and to put his own son-in-law in a safe and high position. But Dreedle does feel that a man heroic enough to win a medal can be excused for appearing "out of uniform," and he does condemn Cathcart and Korn for the right reasons. These factors make Dreedle more of a real man and a real Soldier than either Peckem or Scheisskopt, and make us feel sorry when Dreedle falls victim to their unmanly schemes.

Duckett, Nurse

Note that her vacillation shows a person in the grip of conflict between internal desire and external consideration: (1) she reports Yossarian for making a pass at her, then (2) has a happy affair with him, but (3) recovers her "social sanity" and decides to marry a doctor for financial security. Although he has a huge cast, Heller invests each character with some such pathos.

Dunbar, bombardier

He reinforces both (1) **themes** and (2) plot. When Yossarian describes him as "one of the finest, least dedicated men in the world," we have (1) one of the main points of the story summed up: "dedication" can so blind men to what they are doing that they become inhuman. Dunbar, like Yossarian, never lets the means subvert the ends. Dunbar's protest over orders to bomb undefended civilians - and his subsequent dropping of the bombs into an unpeopled road - (2) prefigures Yossarian's desertion.

Ferredge, Doctor

His name, which means iron-edge, "tags" him (in the classical manner of **black humor**). He is a medical doctor who holds dreams, dreamers, and dream-analysts all in equal contempt.

Flume, Captain, public relations officer

One of the most surrealistic figures in the novel, on many counts: he lives in terror of the Red Indian's revenge on the white man, which is ironical because in his official work, Flume probably attacks the genocidal character of German fascism; but in his awe of some great impending event, Flume reminds the Chaplain of the "voice in the wilderness," a prophet who foretells the coming of one greater than himself, and who therefore calls for a "straightening of the road!" Flume's name means, literally, an "artificial channel for a stream," a reflection probably on his dual role as publicist and prophet. Flume is an extreme example of the way the Black Humorist is likely to describe a character strictly in terms of his effect on others.

Gus And Wes, medical orderlies

They are interesting to the student of Heller on three counts. (1) They symbolize the militaristic tendency to treat human beings as mechanisms: they are ex-mechanics who use assembly-line and computer-like (Yes or No) techniques in diagnosis. (2) They personify Doc Daneeka's callousness as a physician, for he allows them to do his work. (3) They exemplify Heller's technique of pairing characters, especially evil ones, probably to show that in their sinister concurrence, they become indistinguishable from each other. There is something that excludes other people in a team like Gus and Wes or Piltchard and Wren.

Havermeyer, a lead bombardier

Heller uses him as extreme contrast for both Yossarian and Dunbar. Havermeyer so loves destruction that he lingers in violent situations to savor every last bit, even though that endangers the lives of his fellow airmen; this is the polar opposite of Yossarian's "evasive action," intended to accomplish the mission swiftly and escape without casualties. In the briefing for the surprise bombing of the undefended village, Havermeyer anticipates the military aspects with relish, while Dunbar is appalled by the humanitarian considerations. Note that Heller adds two strokes of genius to this harsh caricaturization: Havermeyer spends his off-duty time baiting and shooting field mice, and at the briefing, Colonel Korn tucks his prize warrior under the chin in a way that suggests he's like a hunting dog.

Hungry Joe, veteran combat flier

In his characterization of Hungry Joe, Heller apparently intends to show how the repressive sexual mores of our society predispose a man to accept undue hardship in war. Joe obviously has been brought up to believe that sex is dirty; he can never enjoy any sexual pleasure without feeling guilty. Hence every time Joe qualifies for rotation to noncombat, the very anticipation of such pleasure gives him guilty nightmares. The nightmares end as soon as Colonel Cathcart cuts short his pleasurable contemplation and sends him back to combat: once again, as he expected, he is punished for even daring to hope for consummation. Apparently he is grateful to be saved from his own "dirty" and unworthy expectations. He has been thoroughly conditioned to fear what he wants most: freedom and self-expression.

Korn, Lieutenant Colonel

Like "Doc" Daneeka, Korn practices a profession strictly for selfish ends: he is a lawyer who specializes in how to evade the law. Like Milo Minderbinder and Mrs. Daneeka, Korn knows how to exploit the chaos of war: he is engaged in currency manipulation and black market speculation. Like the Chaplain, he has a good knowledge of psychology, but while the Chaplain uses his for humane purposes, Korn uses his to manipulate people. Theoretically, Korn is Cathcart's subordinate, but in actuality, Korn uses Cathcart as a "front." The most horrifying thing about Korn is that we know the world at large finds him admirable, because he has style. Heller's ability to suit action and language to character are nowhere better demonstrated than in those scenes in which Korn takes over (the briefing for bombing the undefended village; the conference over the loss of Kraft Ferrara). Note that one reason we feel Dreedle has some integrity is that Korn sickens him.

Luciana, a "pickup" in Rome

In some respects, she serves as a strong contrast to Aarfy and as a female counterpart of Yossarian. Her frank, healthy sexuality is contrasted with Aardvark's sanctimonious prudishness and queasy impotence. In her insistence on truth, integrity, and individual dignity, even amid the chaos and corruption of war, she resembles Yossarian. Indeed, in both her name and her action, she symbolizes light, clarification (as when she enters his dark room, flings open the shutters to admit sunlight, and tidies up the place before she can relax into love making!). Note how Heller uses Luciana to further the characterization of Yossarian: she correctly predicts that he will feel such triumph at having had a beautiful woman for nothing that he will undervalue her and throw her address away. But he suffers when he realizes the shallowness of his own attitudes compared to her depth and perspicacity. The portrait of Luciana is the work of a talented painter. She elicited from Heller his most colorful vocabulary, his most sensitive rhythms, his best command of mood. No one will be surprised to hear that (as Heller told this writer in a special interview) Luciana is modeled after a vibrant personality he himself had observed in Rome.

Major Major Major Major, squadron commander

"Who promoted Major Peress?" was a political battle cry during the Fifties when certain "loyalty crusaders" demanded to know why the Army had raised Doctor Peress, a dentist and an admitted leftist, from Captain to Major. From this political cause celebre, Heller developed one of his most farcical yet most pathetic characters. Heller's answer is that the man was promoted by a machine. It makes no difference whether we take it literally to be an IBM machine or metaphorically to be a huge military machine: the promotion was a routine mechanical act. And of course, Heller's Major is also a victim of political cross-fire generated not by "loyalty" but by power-madness. Probably the relationship between Major Peress and Major Major ends right there. But even up to this point the parallel is an interesting illustration of one of Heller's methods of creating characters and situation.

In addition to symbolizing the effects of machine-generated errors and of political cynicism, the story of Major Major's life also strengthens Heller's attack on corruption in American institutions and dramatizes again the breakdown in communication. Major Major's self-aggrandizing father-who could think of no better way to name his son than to give him the family name as first and middle names too - is probably the greatest caricature in American letters of the self-righteous, self-reliant, anti-socialist farmer who grows rich on public subsidy. And Major Major's gradual withdrawal from human relations is almost allegorical in its progress: he is isolated from his friends by being put into the hateful position of commander; he is overwhelmed with self-multiplying administrative memoranda; he is further alienated by Captain Black's spiteful "crusade." Having endured all the frustrations a modern man can suffer in his efforts to relate to his fellow men, he withdraws into his tiny trailer (obviously, retreats into the womb).

McWatt, combat pilot

Heller uses McWatt to show how war fosters wanton disregard of life and to further develop Yossarian's character. This relationship, like all relationships woven through the narrative, develops dramatically. Yossarian's resentment over McWatt's buzzing grows until they come to grips over it in a plane hedge-hopping down a mountain; with abrupt shift of mood, Yossarian is made to feel guilty over the fuss he has made! Then, after McWatt accidentally slices Kid Sampson in half, it is Yossarian who senses that McWatt will kill himself and who races down the beach in a futile human effort to stop him. McWatt seems like a lovable boy who would play with any apparatus, no matter how lethal, as a kind of assertion of potence; pathetically, he matures, judges and executes himself all in a few minutes. By contrast,

Yossarian demonstrates his manhood not by his control over terrifying mechanical power but by his effectiveness in human relations.

Minderbinder, Milo, mess officer

Symbolic of all soldiers who are not above making a profit out of war, Minderbinder is the most single-minded, most monolithic, most frightening character of *Catch-22*. The intense characterization begins with his name. Milo was a Greek athlete who once carried a four-year old cow into the stadium, slew it with one punch to the head, and ate it all in one day. "Minderbinder" continues the description, for while he minds everybody's business for his profit, he binds their minds so they are helpless to protest. Skillfully, Heller shows how the slogans of capitalism (an economic system) are made to sound inextricable from the tenets of democracy (a political system). Milo's bombing his own squadron is abominated until he opens his books and shows that he made a profit - then it becomes a glorious victory for private enterprise! Again Heller uses **anachronisms** to extend his meaning into the post-war world. When Milo says, "What's good for M & M Enterprises is good for the country," he is "echoing" what one of General Eisenhower's Cabinet members said in the Fifties: "What's good for General Motors is...." And again Heller uses contrast in characterization. For Milo can think of nothing but business, he must fight frantically harder and harder to prevent his "gains" from slipping into "losses." Meanwhile, his buddies enjoy love, human companionship, travel, the beach, a good laugh. And while Milo is demanding combat credit and even medals for flights made by other men (since his business deals don't give him time to fight for decorations in his own name!), Dobbs and Nately plunge to a fiery death over La Spezia. The horrifying thing about Milo is that he honestly and sincerely sees nothing unethical in any of his activities.

MUDD, AIR CORPS OFFICER

One of two characters used by Heller to demonstrate that in a bureaucratic system, records are more real than people. Never able to "sign in" to the 256th, because he was rushed into combat as soon as he arrived and was brought back dead, Mudd is officially in limbo, whereabouts officially unknown. The exact opposite is the case with "Doc" Daneeka, for his name was entered on a flight manifest but he didn't go; when the plane crashes he is presumed dead. The point is thus unforgettably dramatized that bureaucratic red-tape creates Life-in-Death and Death-in-Life.

NATELY, AIR CORPS OFFICER

Nately demonstrates the relationship between two of Yossarian's best epigrams: "He had a bad start. He came from a good family" and "war liberates men from the pernicious influence of their families." Ironically, Nately's family - one of power, position, and prestige - sent him into the war only because they thought it would be a short war and would further his career. Note that in his liberation, Nately finds love and a bride-to-be in a relationship he could never acknowledge to his family, and almost - before his death - comes to understand the true nature of his seemingly virtuous father. Note too that "Nately" is one of many "tag" names in *Catch-22*, suggesting not only the family's aristocratic pride in blood-descent (a natal matter) but also the nates (buttocks) which Nately nattily attires.

NATELY'S WHORE

She is Heller's main vehicle for exploring the pathos and paradox of woman's role in a male-supremacist society. Reduced by prostitution to a mere object, she is never able to experience real feelings until she gets a good night's sleep: thus reborn as a person, she realizes she does return Nately's love! Then she runs into the other predicament of being not public property but private property, that is to say, an object again! Ironically, her delayed-reaction to Nately (a good **satire** on the **theme** of waking up to love too late!) catapults her almost at once into the role of bereaved widow! Her antagonism toward Yossarian, the bringer of the bad news, is the fundamental reaction of woman victimized by a man's world: for war is a man-made institution, and once again, Yossarian serves as Everyman! Note too her insight into the relationship between violence and sexual passion, another manifestation of male supremacy, an insight by which she almost undoes poor Yossarian! In her fanatic and persistent tracking of Yossarian, she makes of him a permanent symbol of man's injustice to woman, a guilt Yossarian cannot rid himself of in any male-supremacist society such as Italy's or America's but - and this is significant - maybe can cleanse himself of in a more egalitarian society like Sweden's.

NATELY'S WHORE'S KID SISTER

She symbolizes the younger generation, which of course suffers most from the chaos of war: an orphan, a person who has had no childhood, catapulted prematurely into the worst aspects of adult life. The Establishment, concerned exclusively with the "adult" business of war, has in effect ignored her generation; significantly, only the "drop-out," Yossarian is concerned with her future.

OLD MAN

One of Heller's mythopoeic figures, he identifies himself as Satan, the Antagonist of God, when he attacks Major _____ de Coverley. While Satan and God traditionally compete for men's souls, the Old Man (who runs a public house) and the Major (who sets up a private house) compete for men's souls and bodies. The Major, we noted, is both Hebraic and Hellenistic in his godlikeness, and the Old Man is Hebraic and Hellenistic in his deviltry. Surrounded by the naked women, he is of course Proteus, the Old Man of the Sea, flanked by his sea-cows or mermaids. The Old Man's adaptability alone would tell us this: pro-fascist under Mussolini, pro-Nazi under the Germans, and now pro-democratic under the Americans, the lecherous Old Man is protean. He is capable of myriad superficial and illusory changes because deep down he is always an immutable essence. His age gives him the right to be above wars, dogmas, even nationalities, for living so long in Italy he has seen that all categories, criteria, and boundaries are ephemeral, man-made, illusory. He knows everything because he believes in nothing transitory. Note the great **irony** in the fact that the lecherous Old Man who has no "values" reminds Nately of his own father who represents decent, traditional values. Here are Hegel's interpenetrating opposites for young Nately to blink at! Note the equally staggering **irony** in the Old Man's demise: this eternal cynic, who can be shocked by nothing in the cynical Old World, collapses in the face of American immorality.

ORR, COMBAT PILOT

Almost the real "hero" of the book, Orr is certainly the real "prophet," for it is he who prepares the way for the main character. From the beginning, he has been Yossarian's double, but in a psychoanalytic sense: Orr is the Ego in the partnership, while Yossarian is the Id. Orr plans, directs, relates objectively and rationally to their predicament, while Yossarian by comparison protests and appeals and wallows in subjectivity and inchoateness. This has been symbolized from the beginning, when Orr was the cool brain in the tent-making and Yossarian supplied the brawn and the moodiness. Orr is Yossarian's alter ego. Yossarian's failure to see that in time is exactly analogous to Nately's whore's failure to feel her own feelings before it is too late.

The name Orr is a stroke of genius. For Orr is not only the one who discovers the alternative, the OR, long before Yossarian does. He is not only OmaR the tent-maker. He is also the real Odysseus, the man with the OAR. Like Odysseus, he is resourceful and wily; he has lived among his enemies in disguise (as the wisecracking nonentity with nothing serious on his mind!) while plotting his revenge; he goes off on a pilgrimage with his oar in hand, looking - like Odysseus - for that land of peace.

PECKEM, GENERAL, SPECIAL SERVICES

An important, well-conceived character, he sums up - in action and personality - many of Heller's main points about the relationship between power struggle, cynicism, and communications. He is a larger version of Colonel Korn, as the very relationship between their names will show. They are both concerned with the pecking order. Notice how, in Heller's ingenious plot, Peckem's long-range plans cancel themselves out. He conspires, on the one hand, to get the job of General Dreedle, combat commander. He campaigns, on the other hand, to have combat operations placed under his own Special Services. Apparently, though, these are two alternative ways of getting the same thing (Peckem's advancement): he did not expect both to go through! After he succeeds in his first plan, the alternative also materializes, and he comes out once again on the second rung. Actually, he is worse off, because the man under him whom he left in charge of Special Services now comes out over him. This is splendid **satire** on the endless repetitiveness of power struggles.

The cynicism inheres mainly in the fact that these men are being paid to fight the enemy but actually are fighting each other. While General Dreedle is at least honest enough to concentrate on the legal enemy (the German armies), Peckem and Scheisskopf take advantage of the situation to concentrate on an illegal enemy (Dreedle). How much of a nation's resources, in money and manpower, is wasted in such internal struggle is one of the **themes** of war literature from *The Iliad* to *Othello* to *The Naked and the Dead*. Militarists may actually yearn for war - any war will do - to increase their power over their own countrymen!

Of course, the communications media are essential in Peckem's campaign against his compatriots, and like Korn, Peckem must be much concerned with style. Cynicism has no content; it must impress with suavity and flourish. That is why ex-PFC Wintergreen can keep General Peckem so worried, because Wintergreen affects a knowledge of style. Needless to say, Wintergreen joins Minderbinder because real power manipulators operate outside the official lines of power.

PILTCHARD AND WREN

Heller likes to present his evil characters in pairs, as though to make it clear that their evil (1) makes them indistinguishable from each other and (2) makes them a well-contained society that excludes others. Gus and Wes, as we have seen, are such a pair, with even interchangeable names. Piltchard and Wren represent another form of evil, a kind of evil by default. Heller's description of them reminds us of Alfred Kazin's remark that "War is still the one 'big' experience that the common man will have in his life." And these men are ultra-common: a pilchard is a common sardine, and a wren is a common brown bird. What makes Piltchard and Wren so pathetic is that apparently life offers them no other opportunities so attractive as war.

SAMPSON, "KID," COMBAT PILOT

He typifies Heller's careful attention to every last detail. Heller needed a name for the pilot who is deliriously happy when Yossarian orders him to quit the squadron, abandon the mission, and return to the base. So Heller called him Sampson, and has the "Kid" nickname himself Admiral. Why? Probably because Admiral Sampson was credited with destroying a Spanish squadron in 1899 even though he was not present at the battle. Notice too that Sampson's death as the result of McWatt's buzzing splatters Sampson all over the beach, like so much garbage, and in this respect prefigures the description of the death of Snowden.

SANDERSON, MAJOR, PSYCHIATRIST

He is a conglomerate of all the weaknesses of old-fashioned psychoanalysis, and Heller's criticism of these weaknesses actually anticipates some major reforms within psychoanalysis itself. Sanderson is obviously a man who went into psychiatry in order to study his own psychic disorders, in itself a healthy step, but he also obviously has never been cured! He quickly loses control of the psychiatric interview and becomes, in effect, Yossarian's patient (a good spoof of Freud's countertransference)! He is that pathetic kind of psychologist who uses his professional knowledge to assert "superiority" over the patient. But worst of all, he acts on the orthodox view that any deviation from the "normal" is evidence of maladjustment: failure to conform is neurotic! Thus Yossarian is "immature" because he cannot adapt to arbitrary authority and outmoded tradition. Heller's implicit criticism here adumbrates the attitude of more progressive psychoanalysts (like Rollo May and R. D. Laing) who feel that at a time in history when the Establishment itself is sick, non-conformity may be the only road to psychic health. And Heller is asking a question that Mailer also poses in "The White Negro": what happens when the patient is smarter than the analyst? For that is clearly the case in Yossarian's relation with Dr. Sanderson!

SCHEISSKOPF, LIEUTENANT (COLONEL, GENERAL)

He is an extreme caricature of the most infantile aspects of the militaristic (as distinguished from the military) mind. In his emphasis on precision parading, Scheisskopf wants of course to reduce people to automatic mechanisms, with himself pushing the buttons. In court-martialing Clevinger for making recommendations for improvement of cadet morale (which Clevinger was asked to do!), Scheisskopf personifies a militaristic tendency to repress initiative and foster utter conformity. In performing at Clevinger's trial as both prosecutor, judge, and defense counsel, Scheisskopf serves as a symbol of harsh authoritarian justice. Heller reinforces his caricature by contrasting Scheisskopf with his wife. She is fun-loving, outgoing, sensual; he is grim, single-minded, and has lost sight of the ends for the means. That the power struggles have pushed the most cowardly and irrelevant man to the top of the pyramid is, of course, one of the final ironies of *Catch-22*. Non-combatant by principle, preference, and personality, Scheisskopf is totally incapable of the kind of respect that Yossarian, Dunbar, and Danby need and deserve.

SOLDIER IN WHITE

Probably the master symbol of the novel, he "grows" on the reader. Our first impression is likely to be that he is an extreme case of the mechanical regulation of a human life. But, like the patients in the ward, we also come to feel restless with the facelessness, the self-containment, the withdrawal and isolation of the man. Finally, and again like the patients, we begin to suspect that he is some sort of listening device, some apparatus for recording the talk of the men. Of course, he could have been originally a real patient who gave the "agents" the idea for a "plant." Certainly he is a clever projective device on the part of the author. We use the Soldier in White as the means on which we focus our feelings. For example, the circularity of his life seems like a paradigm of the structure of the book, if not of life itself in a world controlled by Catch-22.

SOLDIER WHO SAW EVERYTHING TWICE

Suffering from fatal damage to the brain, this soldier is just as symbolic of his world as the Soldier in White is. But he plays a more provocative role in the plot. Because of him, we discover the extent of Yossarian's willingness to escape military duty; also, as a punishment for his malingering, Yossarian is forced to act out a death-bed scene for the dead man's family, a comic prefiguring of Yossarian's tragic Descent into Hell later on. The soldier's "seeing everything twice" is also a variation on the **theme** of paramnesia and a musical reinforcement of the overall pattern of the story, which spirals over every event more than once.

TAPPMAN. SEE CHAPLAIN

Texan

This walking self-contradiction helps establish the **themes** of the novel. He is racist and anti-democratic, yet he has a great need for companionship. His compulsive talking drives malingerers out of the hospital back into combat. One reason, surely, is that they are suspicious of sustained discourse. Another, possibly, is that his fascist attitudes remind them of the hypocrisy of the national war aims.

WHITCOMB, CORPORAL, CHAPLAIN'S ASSISTANT

In a novel mainly about officers, Corporal Whitcomb demonstrates how an authoritarian system fosters petty rivalries, truculence, and sinister alliances right down to the lowest grades. The corporal has no intrinsic interest in his job (personally, he's an atheist) but it represents his one chance of "getting ahead." He also has no sincere interest in writing to the next of kin of men killed in action; his form letter - a cynical travesty on "personal" expression of grief - is another indication of the trend toward the mechanization of life. The blatantly careless form in which the letter reaches Mrs. Daneeka is inevitable; it was not intended for "next of kin" at all but for advancement of Whitcomb and Cathcart. Notice the malevolence with which the C.I.D. man, Cathcart, and Whitcomb all focus on the Chaplain. The pressures of authoritarian life require that each of them find scapegoats. Not a bit of their hostility toward the Chaplain seems justified ... except that he is one man who will not threaten them in return.

WHITE HALFOAT (CHIEF), ASSISTANT INTELLIGENCE OFFICER

His presence in the Air Force is a reminder of the **irony** in the American war aims. The United States is fighting the Fascist powers because they break treaties, conquer peaceful peoples, herd certain groups into concentration camps, and engage in genocide. White Halfoat's stories about his people remind us that white Americans have perpetuated all four crimes against the Red man. Halfoat's fear of death by pneumonia is real and realized: suffering from malnutrition in concentration camps called "reservations," American Indians expect to die young of pulmonary disorders. Halfoat's effect on Captain Flume symbolizes the white man's guilt feelings toward the Indian: Flume would of course be most susceptible because as the public relations officer, he has doubtless written a great deal about the "unique" crimes of the Nazis and Fascists.

WINTERGREEN, EX-PFC (EX-CORPORAL, EX-SERGEANT)

His very name indicates his determination to survive like an evergreen shrub, through winter as well as summer. And his preoccupation - and continual association - with T. S. Eliot further indicates his concern with individual survival in a world in collapse. Wintergreen has spent a great deal of time digging holes, reminding us how, in Eliot's *Waste Land*, "Winter kept us warm covering earth," when life could be preserved in minimal fashion as "dried tubers." Significantly, by the end of

Catch-22, Wintergreen is allied with Milo Minderbinder, whose name is also linked with *The Waste Land.* When Eliot opens with the stunning statement that "April is the cruelest month," he means that the month of renewal can be viewed only with mixed feelings by a dying culture. When Heller opens a chapter with the pronouncement that April had been the best month of all for Milo, he invites us to see that Milo is thriving on the chaos. Minderbinder increases and exploits the confusion in commerce; Wintergreen contributes to, and exploits, the breakdown in communications.

Their efforts at survival must be contrasted with the efforts of Orr and Yossarian. The two "manipulators" of commerce and communications are growing rich on human misery, in which they have a vested interest. The two "dropouts" are seeking a clean new world, a fresh start where "the people are so advanced."

WREN

See Piltchard

YOSSARIAN. CAPTAIN, BOMBARDIER

A man who loves life, culture, travel, and adventure, he is cursed with such a sensitivity to injustice, irrationality, and inhumanity that he ultimately finds himself in opposition to all the powers-that-be. He is slow to realize the full implications of his predicament, but when he does, he has the clean courage to take the only definitive action still open to him. Actually his long delay in taking this decisive step serves Heller's purposes perfectly because it gives the author time to make a complete survey of the system that Yossarian, in all self-honesty, must reject.

Yossarian is such a fully developed and complex character that it is worthwhile to study him from many different angles. We can see him as one of the great "drop-outs" in American literature, as a major example of the "anti-hero," as Everyman. We can understand him in terms of the System that he rejects, in terms of his alter ego and of other characters with whom he interacts. All of these are important considerations in arriving at a satisfactory statement about Yossarian's "own personality."

CATCH-22

CRITICS CATCH ON TO CATCH-22

INITIAL REACTION

As Israel Shenker sums it up: "When *Catch-22* came out in October 1961, it was promptly flailed as disorganized, unreadable, and crass." *The New York Times Book Review* dismissed it "for want of craft and sensibility." The staid, academic *Virginia Quarterly* called it "an amateur literary fantasy ... occasionally humorous, often repetitious, usually laborious ..." The anonymous *Virginia Quarterly* reviewer observed that Heller's techniques illustrated his title, "which ... appears to mean one has a right to do anything one can get away with."

Some early reviewers admitted liking the book themselves but willy-nilly took pains to discourage the general reader. For example, William Barrett, writing in *Atlantic Monthly*, almost qualified his praise out of existence:

The book is mostly very funny and exciting to read and I suppose one ought to accept such rare offerings without cavil; but Mr. Heller's talents for comedy are so considerable that one gets irritated when he keeps pressing ... he has a tendency to carry it so far that it becomes mechanical. There is a difference ... between milking a joke ... and stretching it out till you kill it. Mr. Heller has enough verve not to have to try so hard to be funny.

RECOGNITION BY ALGREN

But there were a few scattered critics blessed with that rare ability to recognize a major work of art almost at first sight. Novelist Nelson Algren, writing for the *Nation*, described Heller's novel as "the strongest repudiation of our civilization, in fiction, to come out of World War II." Then he drove that home, hailing *Catch-22* as "not merely the best American novel to come out of World War II, but "the best American novel that has come out of anywhere in years."

BRUSTEIN'S CRITIQUE

And to another perceptive critic, Robert Brustein, goes credit for what may be called the first full-scale critique of *Catch-22*. His essay-length study. "The Logic of Survival in a Lunatic World" (*New Republic*, November 13, 1961), unhesitatingly welcomed Heller as "one of the most extraordinary talents now among us." He substantiated this judgment with enthusiastic description of the characters, insightful explanations of Heller's **themes** and purposes, and telling comparisons of Heller with Norman Mailer, Saul Bellow, and J.P. Salinger.

Brustein correctly identified the critical problem and anticipated the kind of negative criticism that *Catch-22*, by its very nature, would invite.

Considering his indifference to surface reality, it is absurd to judge Heller by standards of psychological **realism** (or, for that matter, by conventional artistic standards at all ...). He is concerned entirely with that thin boundary of the surreal, the borderline between hilarity and horror, which, much like the apparent formlessness of the unconscious, has its own special integrity and coherence.... Heller often manages to heighten the macabre obscenity of total war much more effectively through its gruesome comic aspects than if he had written realistic descriptions.

Brustein expected that Heller would be clobbered by thinkers like Sidney Hook, who had said that any "man who declares that survival at all costs is the end of existence is morally dead, because he's prepared to sacrifice all other values which give life its meaning." Brustein was happily prepared with an illuminating rebuttal:

... contrary to the armchair pronouncements of patriotic ideologues, Yossarian's obsessive concern for survival makes him not only not morally dead, but one of the most morally vibrant figures in recent literature - and a giant of the will beside those weary, wise, and wistful prodigals in contemporary novels who always accommodate sadly to American life (italics ours).

Himself no mean prophet, Brustein also sensed that thorough exegesis of *Catch-22* would reveal certain crucial parallels to Dante's *Inferno*. Brustein acknowledged only one serious fault in *Catch-22*: he called the hospital scene near the end "an inspirational sequence which is the weakest thing in the book." Thus Brustein had virtually outlined the work of other critics to follow.

MAILER'S AMBIVALENCE

Perhaps the first wave of criticism from the popular media reached its crest when Norman Mailer's impressionistic essay, "Some Children of the Goddess," appeared in Esquire (July 1963). Mailer described perfectly the ambivalence toward *Catch-22* that so many readers of his generation experienced. He found that of nine books he had read in three weeks, *Catch-22* took me longest to finish, and I almost give it up. Yet I think that a year from now I may remember it more vividly than [James Jones'] *The Thin Red Line*. Because it is an original. There's no book like it anyone has read. Yet it's maddening. It reminds one of a Jackson Pollock painting, eight feet high, twenty feet long. Like yard goods, one could cut it anywhere. One could take out a hundred pages anywhere from the middle ... and not even the author could be certain they were gone. Yet the length and similarity of one page to another gives a curious meat-and-potatoes to the madness; building upon itself the book becomes substantial until the last fifty pages grow suddenly and surprisingly powerful, only to be marred by an ending over the last five pages which is hysterical, sentimental, and walleyed for Hollywood.

Mailer walked away from these "maddening," mixed feelings with a shrug:

Give talent its due. *Catch-22* is the debut of a writer with merry gifts.

MAILER'S COMMENTS RECONSIDERED

Precisely because they come from a hard-working artist who has wrestled continuously - and with great originality - with the problems of structuring prose, Mailer's remarks deserved careful review. Perhaps we should begin with that famous, clever sentence about the "one hundred pages." Unfortunately, it is usually quoted out of context. Note that, after allowing himself that extravagant pique, confessional writer Mailer almost takes it all back: Yet ... meat-and-potatoes Building upon itself, the book becomes substantial ... The itself that it builds on, obviously, includes the notorious one hundred pages. In other words, Mailer acknowledges that a qualitative change emerges from all that yard goods. And a less restless approach would show us why. For any one hundred pages in *Catch-22* is part of a fabric of foreshadowings, free associations, cross-references, subliminal allusions, paired characterizations, and cyclical, cumulative repetitions. No one could take out any one hundred pages without missing them, because every passage affects all other passages.

Apparently, then, Mailer is not unhappy with the internal structure but with the total bulk, the scale of the work. That is an entirely different matter. Presumably one could go through *Catch-22* pruning out this adjective, that phrase, and scattered paragraphs, here and there, without disturbing the nervous system of the book, and thus shrink it somewhat. But one could not remove one hundred consecutive pages without hacking the body the death. In short, if Mailer is right, if *Catch-22* really is too long, it should not be cut, it should be shrunk, with all its parts remaining in their present proportions and relationships to each other.

But why shorten this book at all? This brings us, maybe, to the real reason for Mailer's pique. His concern about either "finishing" a novel or "giving it up" betrays a non-contemporary attitude toward a book: it must be assaulted, mastered in one sweeping operation; it must be readable in one continuous, linear, dramatically unified experience, or else! A reader raised in the Age, of McLuhan is better prepared to read *Catch-22*; he approaches a novel, or any work of art, with fewer preconceptions and greater flexibility. He is not averse to discrete, episodic, overlapping, interrupted-and-then-resumed experiences with art: as a matter of fact, such contact is closer to everyday reality. If long portions of *Catch-22* are best appreciated as comic routines, sketches, "bits," and variations on a **theme**, the young reader will experience them that way, setting his own pace, taking his own breaks, making his own continuity. Certainly he would find it easier to read *Catch-22* piecemeal than to "give it up"!

Did Heller expect his novel might be read in bits? There is good evidence that he did: the almost self-contained, aphoristic comments, which can be digested separately; the frequent "punchlines" that call for laughter, applause, and encores; the numerous, quick sequences of cinematic "shots"; the numerous but brief bursts of dialogue - all these suggest a work that may be experienced in small units. If this is true, it further explains why Heller uses so many repetitions, echoes, refrains, and cross-references: he is providing for the reader who is absorbing the work in spaced-out sessions. Note that Homer was also, at one time, accused of "needless repetition"; we now know that he was reciting his **epic** in short bursts, for an audience likely to call for a passage now and another tomorrow night. And Heller's *Catch-22* is not the first long modern work susceptible to such dishings out. Clearly Joyce's *Finnegans Wake*, Spenser's *Faerie Queene*, even Dante's *Divine Comedy* can, for many readers, be best absorbed in spaced-out sessions. This does not mean that one could improve such a work by removing a hundred pages from the middle.

Actually, many prominent persons report having read *Catch-22* right through. Poet John Ciardi sat up all night to finish it. Sam Melner, president of Liveright Publishers, was on a Caribbean cruise when he picked up *Catch-22* and couldn't put it down until he reached the last page.

We should repeat, however, that Mailer's candid explanations of his own difficulties very accurately express the uneasiness that many readers felt in their first reading of a book like *Catch-22*. One can appreciate Mailer's objection, because it is so humanly expressed; but one is impatient with similar complaints as voiced by Barrett and the *Virginia Quarterly* because they seem not to have been felt through.

PINSKER'S "ETERNAL BOY"

By the mid-60s, the critical and scholarly journals began featuring in-depth studies of *Catch-22*. One of the most provocative was Sanford Pinsker's "The Protest of a Puer Eternis" (or permanent boy), which appeared in *Critique* (Winter 1964–1965). In previous war literature, Pinsker observed, the hero experienced war as a ritual of initiation into manhood.

The key to the attitudes found in *Catch-22* is not initiation, but survival. The issue, however, is deeper. Yossarian not only refuses the traditional journey of learning in manhood, but adopts the attitude of a perennial innocent. The loss of values ... now becomes a black-and-white faith that institutions are "bad" and individualism is "good."

Pinsker sees Yossarian as a later version of Holden Caulfield, adolescent hero of J. D. Salinger's *The Catcher in the Rye*. "Both Holden and Yossarian are 'protest' figures cut from the same fabric that gave birth to America's original literary innocent,

Tom Sawyer." This line of thought leads Pinsker to conclude that "The desire to strongly identify with a puer eternis is probably one of the major reasons that the book has become so popular."

Actually, the real value of Pinsker's essay inheres more in his excellent analysis of Heller's "structural development," in which he gives evidence that disputes Mailer's complaint that you "could take out a hundred pages anywhere from the middle." Pinsker also throws much light on Heller's use of puns, literary allusions, and figures of speech. For example, he sees the "clear fluid" which runs continuously through the Soldier in White as a good **metaphor** "for the circular structure of the book."

Unfortunately, Pinsker's thesis of the puer eternis smacks of the outmoded psychoanalytic stricture that a young man proves his maturation by becoming "reconciled" with his father figures, that is, by adjusting to the demands of society. According to this view - no longer in vogue among leading analysts - the young man who rebels against authority is suffering from an "unresolved" Oedipal complex, and refusing initiation, is doomed to remain immature.

But Pinsker seems to miss the implication of his very own language. Yossarian does not refuse the "journey of learning in manhood," he simply refuses to take the traditional journey prescribed by his "father figures." Granted, it may be true that some readers enjoy *Catch-22* because they think that Yossarian has postponed his adult responsibilities. But it seems more likely that most readers identify with Yossarian because they admire his courage: in his circumstances, it takes more manliness to rebel than to accommodate! Our rat-race society, thriving on artificial conflicts, can seem so unattractive, so irrational to modern youth that - as one critic puts it - they eschew traditional initiation and prefer "de-initiation."

DOSKOW'S "NIGHT JOURNEY"

Minna Doskow comes to Yossarian's defense in her answer to Pinsker, "The Night Journey in *Catch-22*" (*Twentieth-Century Literature*, January 1967). She agrees that Yossarian may be innocent at the beginning of the novel; and she feels that "his belief that he can work within the establishment using their rules for his own ends is incredibly naive." But he does "learn better, and after his symbolic journey to the underworld, represented by his trip through the dark streets of Rome, he comes to a new recognition of the meaning of his experience ..." She does not see his flight to Sweden as an "escape" but as an "alternative," and she emphasizes Yossarian's own formulation of it: "I'm not running away from my responsibilities, I'm running to them." Thus Miss Doskow finds a meaningful pattern of manly action in *Catch-22*, "similar to the archetypal pattern that characterizes classical **epic** or romance." In her extended analysis, she draws informative parallels between *Catch-22*, *The Odyssey*, the *Aeneid*, and especially *The Divine Comedy*. Not only places and events, but Yossarian, Nately's whore, and Nately's whore's sister all take on a Dantesque significance in this inspired and sensitive study.

THE CLASSICAL TREATMENT

In the late Sixties and early Seventies, critics began to treat *Catch-22* with all the honors reserved for an established "major work." They cut purple patches from it and sewed them into sampler quilts called anthologies. They included *Catch-22* in a great variety of surveys of - for example - war novels, anti-heroic literature, "aesthetics of anxiety." They compared it in detail with the classic anti-war novel - *The Good Soldier Schweik* - and found Joseph Heller greater than Jaroslav Hasek. When *Catch-22* was translated into a movie, they compared film with fiction and found film had failed. When Heller wrote a play, they measured his play against his novel and praised the novel. They raised the solemn question of whether Heller's *Catch-22* might transcend our time - that is, attain immortality.

All such projects of course simply express the art-lover's eagerness always to contemplate a favorite work from a new angle, in a different light.

Novelist-critic-playwright Bruce Jay Friedman has assembled samples of the fiction of J. P. Donleavy, Thomas Pynchon, John Barth, Joseph Heller, himself and others all into one book intended to show the reader the many facets of **Black Humor**, as the anthology is called. In his introduction, he compares and contrasts their styles, emerging with some interesting parallels. "If you are alive today," he observes, and stick your head out of doors now and then, you know there is a nervousness, a tempo, a near-hysterical new beat in the air, a punishing isolation and loneliness of a strange, frenzied new kind. It is in the music and the talk and the films and the theater and it is in the prose style of Joseph Heller and Terry Southern.

STERN ON HELLER AND HASEK

While Friedman found that Heller's style had much in common with that of other contemporary satirists, J. P. Stern was tracing the origins of Heller's satirical style back through the works of Hasek and Charles Dickens ("War and the Comic Muse: The Good Soldier Schweik and *Catch-22*." *Comparative Literature*, Summer 1968). Direct influences of Hasek on Heller, Stern concludes, are most obvious

... where the conflict between the military machine and the private person is presented in its crassest and most absurd form. As for instance, in the figure of Lieutenant, then Captain, then General Scheisskopf ... who, like Lieutenant Dub, is mad about parades.... Again the affinities are clear in the lethal double-talk between superior officer and enlisted man ...

Arranging passages from Heller and Hasek in parallel columns, Stern shows that both authors count on "the literal response [as] a man's only way of parrying the assault of the military machine ... a man's own words are his only refuge and far from indomitable strength ..." But the most important parallel, Stern finds, is in "the basic logic on which both novels operate," namely, that "war is meaningless," and that "the social organizations which aim at the prosecution of war and thus at the efficient inflicting of violent death have ... the appearance of rationality ... but ... are, on that same premise, the opposite of normal and rational."

Stern finds (like Pinsker) that Heller's image of the Soldier in White is "a stroke of genius," in Stern's case because it epitomizes this "absurd rationality" of war. Stern's critique also treats neatly of Heller's clever use of **anachronisms** - to damn the Korean and Vietnam wars even more than World War II - and includes a rich and profound characterization of Yossarian.

Stern beautifully sums up the relationship between the Czech classic Schweik and the American classic *Catch-22*:

To compare the two novels is a little like comparing one of those primitive biplanes ... flown in the First World War with the supersonic jets of our age, in which a machinery of considerable complexity and sophistication hides inside a smoothly streamlined fuselage, an exterior that is as efficient as it is deceptively simple.... Yet the streamlined jet is part of a development which begins with the invention of the flying machine ...

SCHULS ON CATHCART

Max F. Schulz finds in *Catch-22* further evidence of a trend that he traces back to Walter Scott and Samuel Coleridge and that he sees broadly ramified today - not only in literature but in related arts. In his "Pop, Op, and **Black Humor**: The Aesthetics of Anxiety" (*College English*, December 1968), Schulz says:

In his portrait of Colonel Cathcart in *Catch-22*, Joseph Heller defines the Angst of the small, aspiring, flattened, big, weak Massenmensch of our century. Although the nemesis of Yossarian, Colonel Cathcart ironically shares with Yossarian the anxiety that afflicts man faced with his own helplessness and insignificance before the diffusion of twentieth-century mass society ...

Cathcart suffers the "day-to-day fret of the social conformist," as Schulz puts it, because he "seeks integration with what forever eludes him." Among the first characters in modern literature to "exhibit these symptoms," notes Schulz, were "the passive heroes of Scott's Waverley Novels," who seek adjustment to, and avoid collision with, bureaucracy and officialdom. Recalling Coleridge's remarks on the world of the Waverley Novels - "All is an anxious straining to maintain life, or appearances ... to rise as the only condition of not falling" - Schulz sees this description as defining "the malaise of Colonel Cathcart's world of the Forties." But Cathcart's anxious straining" is even greater than the Waverley hero's because since Scott's day, the world has drifted faster toward "fragmentation of experience, isolation of the individual, ... and sense of personal inadequacy."

In Schulz's analysis (as in Pinsker's and Stern's), the Soldier in White emerges as a major figure: he symbolizes modern man's fear of becoming a faceless personality.

DRIVER'S PRAISE OF HELLER'S "WORDS"

When Heller's "experimental" play, *We Bombed in New Haven*, was published in 1968, and when the film version of *Catch-22* finally reached the screen in 1970, many drama and film critics obviously welcomed the chance to extend their comments to include Heller's fiction. Reviewing Heller's play ("Curtains in Connecticut," *Saturday Review*, August 31, 1968), Tom F. Driver, author of several important books on drama, exploded: "Heller is great and *Catch-22* is the greatest and *We Bombed in New Haven* a dud of the first magnitude." *Catch-22* was great because when Heller wrote it, "he was himself ...

... its language was substantial ... you could hear, feel, taste, see and smell it.... The words rang in your ears and swam before your eyes and rattled all around.... All this and much more happened because *Catch-22* is a book that is totally committed, as some books are not, to the notion that the whole world is made up of words. ... The imagination that created it is totally verbal imagination, which is what you would have to say about [Joyce's] *Ulysses*, *Finnegans Wake*, [Nabokov's] *Pale Fire*, and a few other very good books of modern times. ... And the trouble with *We Bombed*...is that it does not have any theatrical substance that could be said to be the equivalent of the verbal substance of *Catch-22*.

Driver thought Heller could succeed as a playwright only by writing the old-fashioned kind of literary play, but should not attempt avant-garde drama: "theater theatrical and improvisatory is not...Heller's route. He should return to words," preferably, Driver seemed to pray, in the medium of fiction.

"POWERFUL HOLD ON A GENERATION"

Valuable praise of *Catch-22* as a novel also came from Richard Schickel reviewing *Catch-22* as a film ("One of our Novels is Missing," *Life*, July 4, 1970). The film fails, feels Schickel, because director Mike Nichols and writer Buck Henry "mislaid...the humor that made the novel emotionally bearable and esthetically memorable," and they weakened "the rich matrix of relationships between its characters." And then, in focusing on Yossarian (who was not really that dominant in the book, says Schickel), the filmmakers have erred by viewing Snowden's death as the major cause of Yossarian's rebellion. "To simplify him so radically is to betray him as a human being and to betray that complexity of vision, that vigorous and skillful art, which gave *Catch-22* the powerful hold it has experienced on a generation."

THE TIMES ATONES (AMBIVALENTLY)

Meanwhile, many critics continue to act out, in their own way, the strange ambivalence toward this book first so well expressed by Mailer. *The New York Times Book Review*, apparently to atone for its original dismissal of *Catch-22* "for want of craft and sensibility," ran, seven years later, a lengthy feature by novelist-playwright Josh Greenfeld in which he reviewed the book's career and assessed its future. Will it transcend its own time?

Greenfeld quoted Heller as saying that "*Catch-22* certainly has more meaning in regard to Vietnam than [to] World War II." However, said Greenfeld, "I don't think the novel is as contemporary as it seems...it has aged." His reasoning was that the contemporary spirit is engaged in active protest, while *Catch-22* reminds Greenfeld of the Fifties, "the age of acquiescence." It "remains curiously static," he said, and it is "really a Fifties cop-out."

... the characters are almost all caricatures, in an arrested state, at least up to the point of death, when they seem to dress for the occasion by assuming flesh. And Yossarian himself - the novel's central character and spine - though he appears to be Heller's attempt to create a cosmopolitan "everyman," is really more like a plain nobody. For he essentially lacks bedrock character - hard and individual substance; actions rub against his character rather than his character being the hard cutting edge that delineates actions.

In fact, by identifying with Yossarian the would-be rebel can remain the would-be rebel.

Yossarian falls short of Greenfeld's criteria for a "real rebel" because of his obedience, his commitment to and unwillingness to confront the organization that is out to destroy him (for instance, he cannot lend his sanction to a buddy's proposal to assassinate the C.O.), his personal and non-ideological opposition to war....

Enough! (Who would read that far if it hadn't appeared in the *Times*?) First of all, note that Greenfeld falls into the trap Brustein had warned against earlier: Greenfeld insists on judging Heller by the standards of **realism**, in spite of his obvious concern "entirely with that thin boundary of the surreal..."

Secondly, even on his own terms, Greenfeld errs. He finds Yossarian lacking in heroic fiber because he is "obedient" and does not engage in suicidal enterprises like fighting the whole Army singlehanded or killing the commanding officer. But didn't Heller want to show, even in his main character, that our society deliberately produces squashed, "plain nobodies"? And Greenfeld must have skipped the passages in which Yossarian unsquashes and un-nobodies himself, refuses to fly more missions, goes AWOL to save a child, and then, rather than compromise his ideals in a "deal" with his C.O., deserts. And what is this about "personal and nonideological opposition to war"? It just happens that Heller's main point is that, in a conformist society, personal refusal is the only heroism left. Does that idea fail to qualify as ideological because only one man holds it - for the moment? Were Thoreau and Gandhi "nonideological"? And how is it that *Catch-22* has such a "powerful hold on a generation" of activists if, by identifying with Yossarian, they can only become "would-be rebels"? Is it possible that traditional critical tactics blind the critic to what Brustein and Doskow and others so clearly perceive: that in his situation, Yossarian can be regarded as heroic, and can inspire admirers and followers of "a new morality"? Apparently *Catch-22* confounds even critics otherwise qualified to write first-page (and pages 49, 50, 51, and 53) think-pieces for the *Times Book Review*. Having slipped all over and failed to get any purchase on his subject, Greenfeld abandons the "rationale" of traditional criticism and lamely signs off: "...if I must conclude that it is not a great book....I still think it is a major work." In short, B + for Mr. Heller.

KAZIN ON CATCH-22 AS FUTURISTIC

While Greenfeld finds *Catch-22* outdated, Alfred Kazin, author of several volumes of major criticism, finds Heller's novel horrifyingly futuristic. ("The War Novel: From Mailer to

Vonnegut." *Saturday Review*, February 6, 1971). He sees *Catch-22* as ... really about the Next War, ... a war that will be without meaning. ... The **Theme** of *Catch-22* ... is the total craziness of war, the craziness of all those who submit to it, and the struggle for sanity by one man.... But how can one construct fictional meaning, narrative logic, out of a system in which everyone but the hero assents to madness and willingly poses as mad?... the imminence now of anyone's death by violence ... makes it impossible to "describe war" in traditional literary ways ... Despite the running gags, the telltale quality of *Catch-22* is that it doesn't move; it can't. The buried-alive feeling of being caught in a plane under attack...produces total impotence, the feeling of being unable to move, to escape....

While critics like Greenfeld lament Heller's "failure" to create a traditional "character," critics like Kazin acknowledge the total impossibility of describing modern war in such traditional ways. While Greenfeld wonders why Yossarian doesn't stand like Horatio at the bridge, Kazin senses that even to maintain one's sanity in Yossarian's situation is to be a hero. While Greenfeld sees *Catch-22* as "curiously static," and blames that on Heller; Kazin says the novel "doesn't move," but blames that on the subject-matter. For, he says, "the urgent emotion in Heller's book is every individual's sense today of...being trapped..." in the Next War. While Greenfeld finds the "ending of *Catch-22*... flat and unconvincing," Kazin apparently cannot bear even to consider it: he sees us all left in "horror-cold immobility," unable to follow Orr and Yossarian as they head for that place where "the people are so advanced."

We might well wonder, why do so many critics boggle, one way or another, over the outcome of the story?

CATCH-22

ESSAY QUESTIONS AND MODEL ANSWERS

Question: Critics often refer to *Catch-22* as a "war novel." To what extent are we justified in calling it an "anti-war novel?"

Answer: This reader is left with the impression that for Heller and his hero, World War II began as an idealistic war, with justifiable humanitarian aims, and degenerated into just another self-negating, militaristic crusade. One moral to be drawn from *Catch-22*, apparently, is that because of the very nature of war, even a "good war" will become an evil, extremist enterprise. No matter how noble the ends, the means become identical with the enemy's. Military methods make a mockery of political goals.

This tragic reversal is epitomized and symbolized in the scene in which Dobbs proposes to Yossarian that they assassinate Cathcart because of his illegal treatment of his men. Dobbs is quickly carried away and soon envisions a blood-bath as means outgrow aims. In his understandable desire to punish a guilty commander, Dobbs would soon out - Cathcart Cathcart. Significantly, this dialogue resonates with echoes of a scene in Julius Caesar.

Dobbs' error is a small-scale version of the overall story of *Catch-22*. A democracy has declared war on the fascist powers because they are aggressively anti-democratic, inhumane, and uncivilized. But the American military establishment is repeatedly revealed as itself being anti-democratic and quasi-fascist. Clevinger, believing that Scheisskopf is sincere in asking for suggestions, responds with valid and pertinent proposals. He is punished for his presumption, framed and humiliated in a trial which leaves him with the knowledge that no Nazi will ever hate him as much as his own superiors hate him. Cathcart's contempt for enlisted men, Dreedle's flaunting of his privileges, the scoundrelly way Korn can insist that disagreement with Korn will be construed as disloyalty to the flag, and the sadistic, inhumane Star Chamber tactics of the C.I.D. men all demonstrate that this Army is not defending democracy but undermining it.

Furthermore, the army Yossarian is serving in is not anti-fascist. Captain Black considers a certain corporal to be un-American because he disapproves of Hitler! The Texan and Cathcart both feel free to express racist attitudes, while the tribal history of White Halfoat makes it clear the American people are themselves guilty of genocide.

Scene after scene in *Catch-22* indicates that war so brings out the worst in men that even a pro-democratic army will become anti-humane. War gives free play to the sadistic impulses of Havermeyer, Aardvark, Black. War creates a chaos favorable only to cynical people like Korn and Peckem, exploitative people like Minderbinder, manipulative people like Wintergreen. War allows MP's to perpetrate an arbitrary, illegal act simply because there is no way to stop them. In the name of efficiency, armies can convert people into mechanisms' as typified by the activities of Scheisskopf and the fate of the Soldier in White. The ultimate anti-humanitarian aspect of even a "good war" is dramatized in the decision to bomb an unwarned civilian population in an undefended village, purely for military purposes. Decent people like Dunbar must, at this point, see no difference between the enemy command and their own command.

An odd and significant fact about *Catch-22* is that as its furious action unfolds, we almost never see, and hardly even hear about, the enemy! "Peckem's target" is Dreedle, the military court's target is Clevinger, the C.I.D.'s is the Chaplain, Minderbinder's is his own squadron! *Catch-22* leaves the reader with the sobering feeling that the Modern-State, democratic or not, uses war not so much to fight a national enemy as to regulate, or at least intimidate, its own people.

Heller obviously does not intend that we read *Catch-22* as only a World War II novel. His numerous **anachronisms** have the effect of updating the story. It was written during the Korean War and found its greatest popularity during the Vietnam War. We seem justified, then, in saying that *Catch-22* is not only a major "war novel," it is also an all-out artistic statement of the modern anti-war position.

Question: How does Heller use humor to accomplish his artistic ends? Give concrete examples of Heller's use of both humorous language and humorous situation.

Answer: *Catch-22* is very largely rendered in the satirical mode. Therefore humor plays an important part. For **satire** is a literary manner that combines wit, **irony**, and sarcasm to expose and discredit human follies and vices. It is of course the humor that makes the bitter moral palatable. Heller's own comments on this technique are pertinent here. He has said, in effect, that his humor makes you drop your guard for the serious blow to follow. "I wanted," Heller said once in an interview, "people to laugh and then look back with horror at what they were laughing at." The technique is time honored in English literature, reaching one of its greatest uses in Dickens, who makes us laugh so that we will not cry. Heller's verbal wit is so good that it ranks with his use of suspense as one of the main reasons we read on. Each superb "gag" or pun makes us hope for another. And each burst of wit is strictly relevant to the subject matter, giving us not the usual diffuse effect of verbal pyrotechnics but rather a cumulative intensity.

For example, Yossarian says that "Nately had a bad start. He came from a good family." And Dunbar is "one of the finest, least dedicated men in the ... world." And the author observes that "all over the world, boys were laying down their lives for what they had been told was their country."

Such witty remarks remind us how dangerous **cliches** are, for they enshrine traditional beliefs that really need to be reexamined. For, as Nately's history illustrates, it may not necessarily be "good" to come from a "good" family. And Dunbar, it turns out, can grow as a person precisely because he is not dedicated but rather open. And before the novel is over, some of the men are wondering bitterly just how much of their country belongs to them. The fact that so much of their energy is expended in these seemingly anarchic jibes in itself demonstrates that survival has become a matter of focusing on - and rejecting - the next moment.

Heller's comic routines also add to serious message of the book. For example, the hospital mess-hall catches fire, and the field firemen rush over and almost extinguish it, but just then the squadron reappears in the sky and the firemen rush off to standby for crash landings but there are none, so the firemen rush back over to the mess-hall which is now ashes. This little routine, coming as it does in Chapter One, is a symbolic **foreshadowing** of many of the larger developments in the story that all end up with men running around in circles, engaged in meaningless, self-negating activity. It's funny and it's folly, which makes it good satire.

Question: What does Heller accomplish by his extensive use of literary allusions?

Answer: Heller uses overt and oblique **allusions** to many writers and their works as a way of reinforcing both his **themes** and his characterizations.

T.S. Eliot's *The Waste Land* is alluded to continually. We are reminded thereby that ours is a dying culture and that the inhabitants of the Waste Land are hoping for individual survival at best. Yossarian fears death by water, as does the **protagonist** of Eliot's poem, strengthening the characterization of the Assyrian as Everyman.

Wintergreen uses Eliot to show what a cultural desert the military establishment can be. He utters the name "T. S. Eliot" over the telephone, in sudden reply to one of Peckem's inane "memoranda," and starts a chain reaction. No one who hears the name can make anything of it (except, of course, for the first two initials, which is the Army abbreviation for the ultimate military comment). By the 1940s, T.S. Eliot was a by-word in Anglo-American culture, but unheard of among the generals and colonels selected to "lead" the Yossarians, Orrs, and Dunbars. Wintergreen's very name, of course, is a reminder of how in *The Waste Land*, Winter kept us warm if not evergreen.

A wry **allusion** to T.S. Eliot also helps to characterize Milo Minderbinder. "April is the cruelest month" because it reminds the inhabitants of the Waste Land of their infertility and inadequacy. But April is the best month of all for Milo because he thrives on the chaos of a culture in decay. Another sarcastic **allusion**, this one to Alfred Tennyson, further characterizes Milo. In Spring, thought Lord Tennyson, a young man's fancy turns to thoughts of love. But not Milo's. In Spring, his thoughts turn to the tangerine harvest, his current black-market target.

Perhaps the most pathetic **allusion** of all is to Villon. When Yossarian wants to know Where are the Snowdens of yesteryear?

he is raising many questions, adding more variations on the traditional ubi sunt **theme**. First of all, Snowden is dead like last year's snow - and Yossarian is raising the Existentialist questions of how well are we living, we who must die? And why must we die, what is the war all about? But prophetically and romantically he reminds us of that greatest of all outlaws - greater even than Robin Hood - Francois Villon, poet and rebel who lived in constant fear of death at the hands of the police, with whom he fought continually. Like Yossarian's reference to Adam, his **allusion** to Villon reminds us that periodically in history, man must rebel against Authority.

Question: What are the artistic effects of Heller's extensive use of "types" in his characterization?

Answer: A "type" is a character who shows us only one side of his nature. Since his function is to present just one human trait or quality, he usually remains static. He is to be contrasted to the characters in the foreground whom we see "in the round" as they develop and change.

Heller unfolds his novel in three literary modes - satiric, surrealistic, and realistic - and the type serves a function in each mode. The purpose of **satire** is to hold certain vices and follies up to ridicule. The type, who isolates a human trait for us, thus appears in **satire** in his extreme form: as a caricature, with the trait under scrutiny exaggerated out of all proportions. Hungry Joe, for example, is a caricature of that pathetic male who drools publicly after women yet lacks the power to relate to them. Scheisskopf is an extreme caricature of the militaristic mind fixated on precision parading.

Surrealism requires the treatment of fantasy and dream experience as though it were actually happening. In our dreams certain persons are such types as to become archetypes. Aardvark is such an extreme type of sadist as to be nightmarish. Major is such an extreme type of sadist as to be Major __ de Coverley moves through the action like a Divine Father-Figure.

Realism requires objective accuracy, the kind of reporting of events that is basically a recording of outer reality. Types serve their purpose here too. Perhaps Colonel Moodus is a good example of a realistic type. There is often, in real life, the young man who gains high position through his father-in-law's high position.

If we see him in no other light, then we see him as a type, although of course others may see him "in the around." And that does happen to be the main artistic value of the type: he represents the way we see a certain person who relates to us through only one circumstance or quality. In any realistic work with a large cast of characters, most of them must be types because in art, as in real life, we can know only a few people in depth. With his surrealist and satiric requirements added to his realistic needs, Heller actually requires about 40 or 50 types.

Question: How does Heller structure *Catch-22*? What artistic functions does this type of structure serve?

Answer: Heller structures his material - that is, arranges his revelations - in a psychological pattern. The experiences of the 256th Squadron that he wishes to build on are revealed largely by free associations of the characters. Present action evokes recollections of past actions which are then experienced simultaneously with the present, Heller said, in an interview published in Mademoiselle, that he was using here the technique Faulkner had employed in Absalom, Absalom!

We are introduced to this pattern immediately. Heller opens with a few "cute," seductive remarks about Yossarian and the Chaplain. Then, the narrative spirals off on a series of free associations, not returning to the Chaplain-Yossarian situation for four pages. Each chapter, like Chapter One, is strewn with hints of coming attractions. Since some materialize very soon (like the Chaplain-Yossarian bit), we begin to expect that all such hints will pan out. Near the end of Chapter One, we hear about a cetologist who was shanghaied into the Medical Corps because of a faulty anode in an IBM machine. This absurd consequence of a machine error foreshadows a major divulgence that will not occur until 73 pages later. Again, in Chapter Three, Heller calmly mentions in passing the night that Milo bombed his own squadron, an event here recalled as past action but not to be developed in full until many chapters later. Some motifs - like the Snowden trauma - will spiral back into our awareness again and again, with some new development every time.

Thus, a pattern of **foreshadowings** and echoes is set up, reinforced by such symbolic situations as that of the Soldier Who Saw Everything Twice and that of the Chaplain who ponders paramnesia (the delusory sensation that one has experienced present circumstances sometime in the past).

Heller also reinforces his structure with strong contrasts of all kinds: contrasts in mood, setting, characterization. We go from the bloody, fiery, mess over Ferrara to a lovely afternoon on the beach at Pianosa to another shattering combat scene over Bologna. In one chapter, we go from a hair-raising hedge-hopping trip down a mountainside to a romantic interval on the beach to the slicing and splashing of Kid Sampson by fun-loving McWatt.

The artistic validity of this main pattern of recall and juxtaposition of past with present is, of course, that several of the characters are assembling themselves for crisis. Cathcart, for example, has to weigh his own merits and demerits before he can face the general. The Chaplain and Yossarian are both evaluating their past experience in preparation for a great spiritual transformation. The Chaplain is about to become the Scapegoat. Yossarian has to become the New Hero. The greater the self-confrontation, the deeper the probing: hence only near the **climax** can Yossarian re-live the entire Snowden episode.

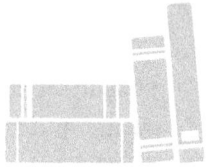

CATCH-22

TOPICS FOR RESEARCH AND CRITICISM

THEMES OF CATCH-22

What They Had Been Told Was Their Country: *Catch-22* and the Question of Patriotism.

The Validity of Heller's Attack on the Mechanization of Modern Man *Catch-22* and the Vietnam War

The Validity of Heller's Attack on Big Business (Medical Profession, Subsidized Agriculture)

A Woman's Reactions to the Man's World of *Catch-22*

Religion and Atheism in *Catch-22*

Catch-22 as a **Satire** on Modern Written and Spoken Communication

Paramnesia, Chaplain Tappman, and *Catch-22*

Catch-22: **Foreshadowing** of R. D. Laing's Psychology

Sadism, Wart, and *Catch-22*

The Police as a Force for Evil in *Catch-22*

Sidney Hook and Joseph Heller: Conflict in Value Judgments

HISTORICAL BACKGROUND OF CATCH-22

"The People Are So Advanced": Sweden in World War II

Ferrara, Bologna, and Avignon: History behind the Action of *Catch-22*

"The Eternal City": A Comparison of Rome in Heller's *Catch-22* and the Historical Rome of 1945

Prostitution in World War II and in *Catch-22*: Is Wartime Sexual License Part of the Appeal of War?

The Assyrian in America: Yossarian's Background?

The B-25 and its Role in *Catch-22*

Black Market Operations in World War II: Background for *Catch-22*

Pianosa: the Fiction and the Reality

Use of the Loyalty Oath in the 1950s" Background for Heller's "Grand Loyalty Oath Crusade"

The Army Nurse Corps in World War II: History Behind *Catch-22*

"Who promoted Major Peress?" The Political Background of Heller's Major Major Major Major

The Chaplain's Corps in World War II: History Behind the Action of *Catch-22*

HELLER'S CHARACTERIZATION

Heller's Portrayal of Women

Captain Flume and the Voice in the Wilderness (Isaiah 40)

Peckem and Fortinbras: Is it a Fair Comparison?

Function of Pairing in Heller's Characterization

Luciana and the "Santa Lucia" Festival of Lights

Heller's Major _____ de Coverley and Addison's Sir Roger de Coverley

The Old Man as Proteus and as Satan

The Texan: Why So-Called? Why Not The New Yorker or The Californian?

The Historical Validity of Heller's Chief White Halfoat

Heller's General Peckem (*Catch-22*) and Mailer's General Cummings (*The Naked and the Dead*)

Orthodox Freudianism and Major Sanderson

YOSSARIAN

Yossarian and Huckleberry Finn

Yossarian as an Existentialist

Yossarian as Everyman

Yossarian's Attitude toward Women

Heller's Yossarian and Vonnegut's Billy Pilgrim: Everyman in the War Novel

Dostoevsky's Raskolnikov and Heller's Yossarian: Was Clevinger Right?

Heller's Yossarian and Shakespeare's Falstaff: Comparison and Contrast

Yossarian and the Good Soldier Schweik: A Comparative Study of Character Development

Yossarian: Anti-Hero or New Hero?

HELLER'S TECHNIQUES

Satire, Surrealism, Realism: Heller's Three Modes

Heller's **Similes** and their Literary and Psychological Impact

Heller's Symbolism

Henry James' Theory of "Point of View": Applied to Joseph Heller's *Catch-22*

Heller's Use of Tag Names: A Critical Analysis

Heller's Use of Poetic Devices: **Metaphor** and Word-Music

Heller's Puns and What They Add to **Theme** and Characterization

Heller's Anachronisms: What They Add to the Message of the Novel

Heller's Use of the Extension an Absurdum Technique

Deus ex Machina in *Catch-22* and in Selected Greek Dramas

Why the Controversy over the Ending of *Catch-22*?

COMPARISONS WITH OTHER WORKS AND OTHER WRITERS

Heller's Place in the Literature of **Black Humor** (see Friedman, "Annotated Bibliography")

J. D. Salinger's *The Catcher in the Rye* and Joseph Heller's *Catch-22*: Comparison and Contrast

Heller's *Catch-22* and Hemingway's *Farewell to Arms*: A Comparison of Themes, Heroes, and Literary Method

The Oar in Homer's *Odyssey* and Heller's *Catch-22*

Heller's *Catch-22* and Homer's *Iliad*: A Comparative Study in the Appeal of War

Anti-Hero in the Fiction of Joseph Heller and J.P. Donleavy

The "Simultaneous Sweep" in Heller's *Catch-22* and Faulkner's *Absalom, Absalom!*

T. S. Eliot's *The Waste Land* as an Inspiration for *Catch-22*

Relevance of the Villon **Allusion** to the **Theme** and Plot of *Catch-22*

The Roman Saturnalia and Heller's "Thanksgiving"

Shakespeare's *Julius Caesar* as Inspiration for **Theme**, Incident, and Dialogue in *Catch-22*

Euripides' *Bacchae* and Heller's *Catch-22*

Heller's Indebtedness to Jaroslav Hasek's *The Good Soldier Schweik*

Heller's Debt to Louis-Ferdinand Celine's *Voyage* au bout de la nuit (Paris, 1932)

Joseph Heller's Debt to Pirandelo: An Examination of *We Bombed in New Haven*

Joseph Heller and Nathaniel West: A Comparative Study of literary Attitudes

Catch-22 and *Slaughterhouse-Five*: A Comparison in Methods and Themes

Catch-22 and *We Bombed in New Haven*: A Comparison in **Theme** and Impact

Joseph Heller's *Catch-22*, Ken Kesey's *One Flew Over the Cuckoo's Nest*, and the Novel of the Absurd

Heller's *Catch-22* and Thoreau's *Civil Disobedience*

Anxiety in the Fiction of Joseph Heller and Bruce Jay Friedman

DISCUSSION OF HELLER'S CRITICS

Is *Catch-22* a "Cop-out of the Fifties"? An Answer to Josh Greenfeld Which 100 Pages, Mr. Mailer?

Pinsker and Doskow: Contrast and Appraisal

Dante, Heller, and Doskow: An Evaluation of Doskow's Approach to Chapters 39–42

BIBLIOGRAPHY

EDITIONS OF JOSEPH HELLER

Catch-22. New York: Simon and Schuster, 1961. Hardcover.

Catch-22. New York: Dell, 1962. Paperback.

Catch-22. London: Jonathan Cape, 1962. Hardcover.

We Bombed in New Haven. New York: Knopf, 1968. Hardcover.

WRITINGS ABOUT HELLER AND HIS WORKS

Algren, Nelson. "So Wild that it Hurts." *Nation* 193 (November 4, 1961), p. 357. Enthusiastic reception by an established novelist.

Barrett, William. "Two Newcomers." *Atlantic* 209 (January 1962), p. 98. Mild praise from the noted Existentialist philosopher.

Brustein, Robert. "The Logic of Survival in a Lunatic World." *New Republic* 145 (November 13, 1961), pp. 11–13. Brilliant and thorough. Describes Yossarian as one who "finds his absolutes in the freedom to be."

Daedalus XCII (1963), pp. 155–165. Truculent criticism, unsigned.

Doskow, Minna. "The Night Journey in *Catch-22*." *Twentieth-Century Literature* 12 (January 1967), pp. 186–193. Imaginative analysis of Chapters 39–42 in terms of the parallels with Dante's *Inferno* and other epics. Refutes Pinsker.

Driver, Tom F. "Curtains in Connecticut." *Saturday Review* 51 (August 31, 1968), pp. 22–24. Ranks Heller the novelist with Joyce and Nabokov, by way of discouraging Heller the playwright. Provocative appreciation of Heller's love of words.

Flagler, J. M. "Mike Nichols Tries the Impossible - A Movie of *Catch-22*." *Look* (June 30, 1970), pp. 55–59. Interesting discussion of problems of conversion to film medium. Stills from film show Nichols' conception of Milo, Nurse Duckett, the apartment of girls, etc.

Friedman, Bruce Jay, Editor. *Black Humor*. New York: Bantam, 1965. A critical anthology that places Heller in a literary "movement" as diverse as it is powerful, with introductory comments by Friedman, himself a Black Humor novelist and playwright.

Greenfeld, Josh. "22 was Funnier Than 14," *New York Times Book Review* LXXIII (March 3, 1968), pp. 1, 49–51, 53. Entertaining, but unreliable on facts and contradictory in arguments. Review of reputation of novel, account of interview with Heller, ending with Greenfeld's judgment of *Catch-22* as "really a Fifties cop-out."

Hoene, Anne; Judith Innes; Victoria Lewis, interviewers. "So They Say." *Mademoiselle* (August 1963), pp. 234–235. Brief but compact and informative account of interview with Heller.

Kazin, Alfred. "The War Novel: From Mailer to Vonnegut." *Saturday Review* 53 (February 6, 1971), pp. 13–15, 36. Sees "static" quality of novel as consequence of horror of subject, the gags as escape from meaning, work generally as "really about the Next War."

Mailer, Norman. "Some Children of the Goddess." *Esquire* (July 1963), reprinted in: Harold Hayes, editor. *Smiling Through the Apocalypse: Esquire's History of the Sixties.* New York: McCall Publishing Co., 1970. pp. 836–838. Valuable first impressions of a moody reader who had trouble finishing the book but admits he won't forget it.

Newsweek. "Heller Cult." 60 (October 1, 1962), pp. 82–83. Good information on popularity of the book one year after publication, sales history, biographical data, etc.

Pinsker, Sanford. "The Protest of a Puer Eternis." *Critique* 7 (Winter 1964–1965), pp. 150–162. While his main thesis is poorly formulated and feebly ramified, Pinsker is provocative on Heller's themes, structure, literary allusions, puns, etc.

Schickel, Richard. "One of our Novels is Missing." *Life* (July 4, 1970), p. 12. Finds that the film version of *Catch-22* simplifies Yossarian so "radically" as "to betray him as a human being and to betray that complexity of vision ... which gave *Catch-22* the powerful hold it has exercised on a generation."

Schulz, Max F. "Pop, Op, and **Black Humor**: The Aesthetics of Anxiety." *College English* 30 (December 1968), pp. 230–241. Germinal discussion of Cathcart's character, related neatly to Coleridge's criticism of Scott and to contemporary trends in the fine arts.

Shenker, Israel. "Joseph Heller Draws Bead on the Politics of Gloom." *New York Times* (September 10, 1968), p. 49. Interview with Heller about his views on Vietnam War: "I loathe it. I detest it. I oppose it."

Stern, J.P. "War and the Comic Muse: *The Good Soldier Schweik* and *Catch-22*." *Comparative Literature* XX (Summer 1968), pp. 193–216. Although he may have overemphasized the "direct influences of Hasek's work on Mr. Heller's," Stern is richly provocative in his study of "three-stages of the associative device" (in Dickens, Hasek, Heller), of Heller's anachronisms, of Yossarian's character, etc. Contains a dozen starting points for new research or critical papers.

Time. "Sustaining Stream." 81 (February 1, 1963), p. 82. Clever review that represents *Catch-22* as great in spite of itself.

Virginia Quarterly Review. "Notes on Current Books." 38 (Winter 1962), p. x. Supercilious brush-off, interesting only as illustrating the queasiness of the traditional mind as it faces an untraditional work of art.

Walters, Raymond. "Catch Cult." *New York Times Book Review* (September 9, 1962), p. 8. Information on the popularity of the book just one week before it went into paperback.

www.ingramcontent.com/pod-product-compliance
Lightning Source LLC
LaVergne TN
LVHW021720060526
838200LV00050B/2769